# Florida Keys Travel Guide 2025

**Unveiling the Diverse Charms of Paradise: Key Largo, Islamorada, Marathon, Big Pine Key, and Key West**

## Glen C. Flores

## Florida Keys Map

4.7 ★★★★★ 1,081 reviews
View larger map

Google
Keyboard shortcuts | Map data ©2024 INEGI | Terms | Report a map error

**Florida Keys**
Florida

4 7 ★★★★★ 1 081 reviews

Directions

# Scan this QR Code

1. Open your phone's camera app.
2. Point the camera at the QR code.
3. Ensure the code is focused and in view.
4. A notification or link will appear.
5. Tap the notification to open the linked content.

Google
Keyboard shortcuts | Map data ©2024 INEGI | Terms | Report a map error

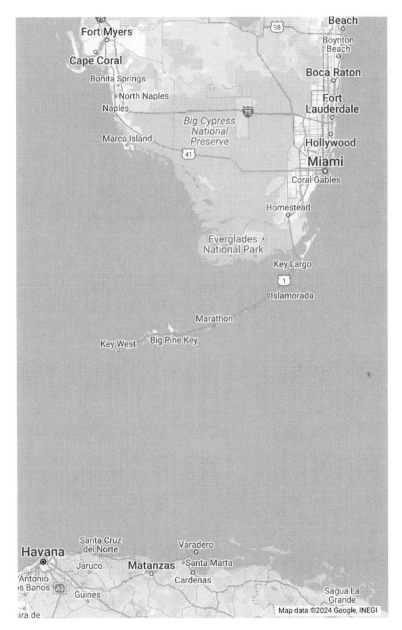

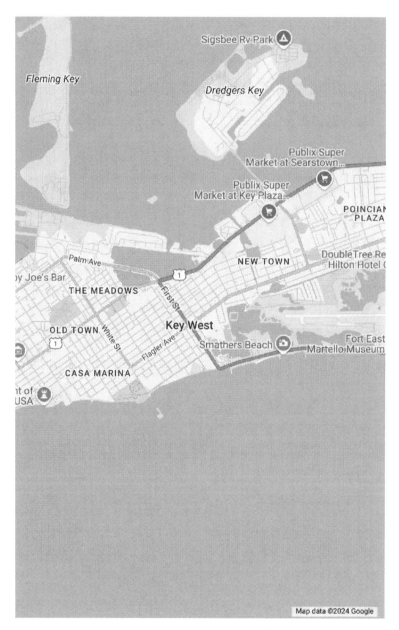

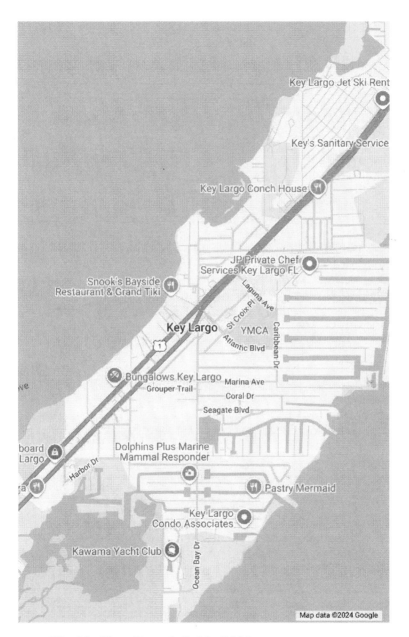

*Florida Keys Travel Guide 2025*                    5

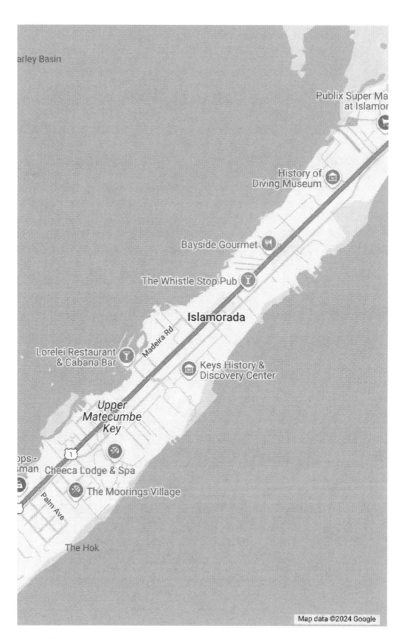

*Florida Keys Travel Guide 2025*

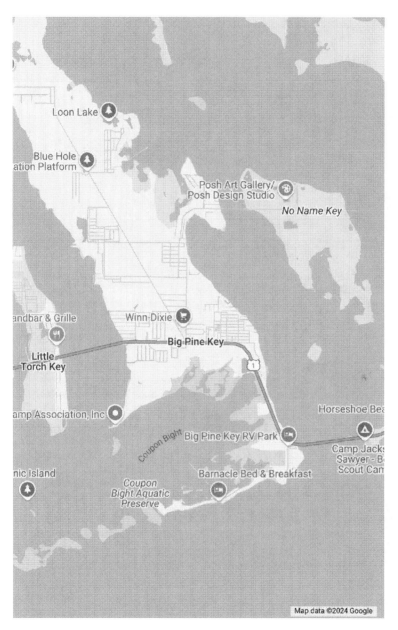

# Table of Contents

# Preface

The Florida Keys. Just the name conjures up images of sun-drenched beaches, swaying palm trees, and a laid-back rhythm that melts away stress. This archipelago, strung like emeralds across the turquoise waters at Florida's southernmost tip, is an escape. Whether you dream of diving into vibrant coral reefs, reeling in a trophy fish, kayaking through mangrove tunnels, or simply soaking up the quirky charm of Key West, this guide is your passport to unlocking the magic of the Keys.

But the Florida Keys are more than just a picture-perfect postcard. They're a tapestry woven from history, nature, and a unique blend of cultures. Pirates once roamed these shores, seeking hidden treasures among the coral cays. Pioneers carved out settlements, leaving their mark on the landscape and the local lore. Today, a spirit of conservation thrives, protecting the delicate ecosystem and the unique wildlife that call the Keys home.

In this guide, we'll journey through each of the major Keys, from the diving haven of Key Largo to the vibrant energy of Key West. You'll discover hidden gems and iconic landmarks, savor fresh seafood and international flavors, and find the perfect accommodations to suit your style. You'll find it within these pages whether you're seeking adventure, relaxation, or a taste of island life.

We'll equip you with the practical information you need to plan your trip, from transportation tips to visa requirements. We'll delve into the diverse attractions each Key offers, from world-class museums and art galleries to thrilling water sports and vibrant nightlife. We created a 14-day itinerary to show you the best of the Florida Keys to maximize your time.

So, turn the page and let this guide be your companion as you embark on an unforgettable journey through the Florida Keys. Discover the diverse charms of this island paradise, create lasting memories, and embrace the spirit of adventure that awaits you. Your Key West sunset celebration awaits.

# Introduction

The rumble of the old Greyhound bus vibrated through my bones, a steady rhythm accompanying the blur of neon signs and strip malls as we sped down the Overseas Highway. I was 22, armed with a backpack full of dreams and a crumpled map of the Florida Keys, a place that had beckoned me with promises of turquoise waters, swaying palms, and a life lived on "island time."

Growing up in a landlocked town, the ocean had always held a mystical allure. I devoured books about Jacques Cousteau, dreamed of coral reefs teeming with life and imagined myself swimming alongside dolphins in crystal-clear waters. The Florida Keys, a string of islands trailing off the tip of Florida like a mermaid's tail, seemed like the embodiment of those dreams.

I went to the Keys to escape the daily grind, but more. It was about finding myself. A recent college graduate with a degree in hand and a heart full of uncertainty, I felt adrift in a sea of expectations. The pressure to choose a career path, to settle down, to conform to the "normal" trajectory of life, weighed heavily on me. I longed for a place where I could shed those expectations, breathe in the salty air, and discover who I truly was.

The Keys, I hoped, would be that place. A place where the rules were different, where life moved at its own pace, and where the vibrant colors of the natural world mirrored the vibrancy of the soul.

As the bus crossed the bridge, leaving the mainland behind, a sense of exhilaration washed over me. The landscape transformed, the urban sprawl giving way to mangroves, swaying palms, and glimpses of sparkling water. With each mile, the air grew thicker with the scent of salt and sea, and the weight on my shoulders seemed to lighten.

My first glimpse of Key Largo took my breath away. The water, a shade of turquoise I'd never seen before, shimmered under the golden sun. Lush green vegetation spilled onto white-sand beaches, and colorful houses dotted the coastline like scattered jewels. It was a world away from the gray concrete and hurried pace of my hometown.

Over the next few weeks, I immersed myself in the magic of the keys. I snorkeled through coral reefs, marveling at the kaleidoscope of colors and the intricate dance of marine life. I kayaked through mangrove tunnels, feeling a sense of peace as I glided through the tranquil waters. I wandered through Key West's bustling streets, captivated by the island's quirky charm and vibrant energy.

I met fishermen with weathered faces and stories of the sea etched into their skin. I chatted with artists who drew inspiration from the vibrant colors of the sunset. I shared laughter and stories with fellow travelers, each of us seeking our own version of paradise.

The Keys, I discovered, were more than just a beautiful destination. They were a melting pot of cultures, a haven for artists and dreamers, and a place where the boundaries between land and sea blurred. It was a place where I could shed my inhibitions, embrace the unexpected, and discover a strength and resilience I never knew I possessed.

As I boarded the bus back to the mainland, a bittersweet feeling settled in my heart. I was leaving a part of myself behind, a part that had blossomed under the warm Florida sun. But I also carried with me a newfound sense of clarity, a deeper understanding of who I was and what I wanted from life.

The Florida Keys, I realized, had given me more than just a collection of memories. They had given me the gift of self-discovery.

Now, years later, as I write these words, the magic of the keys still lingers within me. The scent of salt air, the feel of warm sand between my toes, the sound of waves crashing against the shore—these are the sensations that transport me back to that transformative time in my life.

And so, I invite you to embark on your own Florida Keys adventure. Whether you're seeking adventure, relaxation, or a journey of self-discovery, these islands hold the promise of something extraordinary. Turn the page and let this guide be your compass as you navigate the turquoise waters, vibrant cultures, and unforgettable experiences that await you. Your own Florida Keys story is waiting to be written.

*Are you ready to escape to paradise? Let this guide be your key to unlocking the magic of the Florida Keys.*

# Island Gems

The Florida Keys are a string of islands, each a distinct gem with its own personality and allure. Let's delve into the essence of each major key, uncovering what makes them unique and who they might appeal to most:

**Key Largo:**

- Unique Characteristic: The Underwater Wonderland. Key Largo boasts the only living coral barrier reef in the continental United States, making it a world-renowned diving and snorkeling destination.
- Must-Do Experience: Immerse yourself in the vibrant underwater world of John Pennekamp Coral Reef State Park. Snorkel or dive amidst colorful coral reefs, encounter diverse marine life, and explore the famous Christ of the Abyss statue submerged in the crystal-clear waters.
- Ideal Traveler: nature lovers, divers, snorkelers, kayakers, and those seeking a tranquil escape surrounded by natural beauty.

**Islamorada:**

- Unique Characteristic: The Sport fishing Capital. Islamorada is a haven for anglers, boasting world-class fishing opportunities and a vibrant fishing culture.
- Must-Do Experience: Embark on a thrilling sport fishing charter and try your luck at reeling in a trophy catch. Whether you're a seasoned angler or a novice, the experienced guides and abundant marine life will ensure an unforgettable fishing adventure.
- Ideal Traveler: Fishing enthusiasts, families seeking outdoor activities, those who appreciate fresh seafood and local charm, and anyone looking to escape the ordinary.

**Marathon:**

- Unique Characteristic: The Heart of the Keys. Marathon is centrally located and offers a diverse range of attractions, from historical landmarks to family-friendly activities.
- Must-Do Experience: Drive across the iconic Seven Mile Bridge, a marvel of engineering and a symbol of the Florida Keys. Stop at the scenic overlook for breath-taking views and photo opportunities.
- Ideal Traveler: Families with children, history buffs, those seeking a mix of relaxation and adventure, and anyone who appreciates stunning scenery and diverse activities.

**Big Pine Key & the Lower Keys:**

- Unique Characteristic: The Laid-Back Escape. The Lower Keys offer a tranquil retreat from the hustle and bustle, with a focus on natural beauty and unspoiled landscapes.
- Must-Do Experience: Visit the National Key Deer Refuge and encounter the adorable Key deer, a miniature species unique to this region. Explore the pristine beaches, kayak through mangrove tunnels, and soak up the serenity of island life.
- Ideal Traveler: nature enthusiasts, those seeking tranquility and solitude, kayakers, eco-tourists, and anyone looking to disconnect from the modern world.

**Key West:**

- Unique Characteristic: The Quirky Cultural Hub. Key West is a vibrant island city with a rich history, a thriving arts scene, and a lively atmosphere.
- Must-Do Experience: Stroll down Duval Street, soaking up the eclectic shops, art galleries, and lively bars. Celebrate the sunset at Mallory Square, a nightly tradition filled with street performers and vibrant energy.
- Ideal Traveler: Those seeking a lively and social atmosphere, history buffs, art enthusiasts, LGBTQ+ travelers, and anyone who appreciates a unique and quirky destination.

Each of these Keys offers a unique blend of experiences, catering to diverse interests and travel styles. Whether you're seeking adventure, relaxation, or cultural immersion, you'll find your perfect island gem in the Florida Keys.

## Historical Background

The Florida Keys, an archipelago draped across the turquoise expanse of the Atlantic Ocean, possess a history as rich and diverse as the marine life that inhabits their surrounding waters. From the initial presence of indigenous peoples to the vibrant cultural fusion of the present day, the Keys have borne witness to a compelling interplay of human endeavor, natural forces, and an enduring spirit of exploration.

**Early Inhabitants and Spanish Colonialism:** Long before European vessels traversed these waters, the Keys were inhabited by indigenous tribes, the Calusa and Tequesta, who thrived in this subtropical environment. Adept fishermen and canoe builders, they navigated the intricate network of waterways and mangrove forests, leaving behind shell mounds and artifacts that offer glimpses into their ancient civilization.

The arrival of Spanish explorer Juan Ponce de León in 1513 marked a pivotal moment in the Keys' historical narrative. Driven by legends of a Fountain of Youth, he claimed the land for Spain, christening it "La Florida" in recognition of the Easter season ("Pascua Florida") and its verdant landscape. However, encounters with the indigenous populations proved formidable, and Ponce de León's aspirations for gold and eternal youth remained unrealized.

**A Haven for Buccaneers and the Rise of a Maritime Economy:** The 17th and 18th centuries witnessed the Keys become a sanctuary for pirates and privateers, lured by the treacherous reefs and secluded coves that provided both refuge and opportunities to plunder passing vessels. Legends of Blackbeard and other infamous buccaneers persist, imbuing the islands with a sense of swashbuckling intrigue.

As Spanish dominion waned, intrepid pioneers began to settle the Keys, drawn by the promise of abundant fishing grounds and the lucrative industry of salvaging cargo from shipwrecks. Key West, strategically positioned at the southernmost point, evolved into a thriving port, attracting merchants, fishermen, and those seeking a life on the fringes of civilization.

The 19th century was marked by a struggle for control between Spain and the nascent United States, culminating in Florida's acquisition as a U.S. territory in 1821. This period also witnessed the Seminole Wars, as indigenous tribes resisted forced displacement. The Keys, with their remote location and intricate waterways, provided refuge for both Seminoles and escaped slaves, who forged alliances and fought for their autonomy.

**Bridging the Islands: An Engineering Triumph and Nature's Fury:** A transformative chapter in the Keys' development unfolded with the vision of Henry Flagler, a railroad magnate who envisioned connecting the islands by rail. The Overseas Railroad, an extraordinary feat of engineering, was completed in 1912, linking Key West to the mainland and ushering in an era of enhanced accessibility and economic growth.

However, the resilience of the Keys was tested in 1935 when a catastrophic hurricane, one of the most powerful in U.S. history, ravaged the islands. The railroad was decimated, lives were lost, and the landscape was irrevocably altered. Yet the indomitable spirit of the Keys endured.

**The Modern Era: Tourism, Conservation, and Cultural Fusion:** The aftermath of the hurricane prompted a shift in priorities, with the Overseas Railroad replaced by the Overseas Highway, a scenic roadway that solidified the Keys' connection to the mainland and facilitated the rise of tourism.

Today, the Florida Keys are a globally renowned destination, attracting visitors with their pristine natural beauty, diverse marine ecosystems, and vibrant cultural tapestry. Key West, with its distinctive charm and literary heritage (most notably, Ernest Hemingway's residence), has become an iconic embodiment of the Keys' unique character.

Amidst the flourishing tourism industry, a growing recognition of the delicate ecosystem has spurred conservation efforts aimed at safeguarding the coral reefs, mangrove forests, and unique wildlife that define the Keys. National parks, wildlife refuges, and sustainable tourism initiatives are dedicated to preserving this island paradise for posterity.

The Florida Keys stand as a testament to human resilience and adaptability, a place where history, nature, and culture converge to create a singular and captivating experience. The Keys continue to fascinate and captivate, providing a peek into a world where the rhythm of existence harmonizes with the ebb and flow of the tides, from the ancient presence of indigenous tribes to the modern travelers seeking their own sanctuary.

## Unique Ecosystem

The Florida Keys, an archipelago tracing the southeast edge of the United States, represent a delicate tapestry of interwoven ecosystems. More than just a tropical paradise, these islands harbor a unique confluence of terrestrial and marine environments, supporting a rich biodiversity that demands both admiration and vigilant conservation.

**Submerged Majesty the Coral Reefs:** Often hailed as the "rainforests of the sea," the coral reefs of the Florida Keys constitute the third-largest barrier reef system globally. These submerged havens teem with life, providing shelter and sustenance for a dazzling array of marine organisms. From the intricate branching structures of elkhorn coral to the vibrant hues of brain coral, these underwater cities are constructed by tiny polyps, creating a foundation for an entire ecosystem.

The reefs' significance extends beyond their aesthetic beauty. They act as natural breakwaters, mitigating the impact of storms and coastal erosion while also serving as vital nurseries for commercially important fish species. The economic vitality of the Keys is intrinsically linked to the health of these reefs, underscoring the need for their protection.

**Coastal Guardians the Mangrove Forests:** Fringing the islands' edges, mangrove forests stand as sentinels between land and sea. These remarkable trees, adapted to thrive in saltwater environments, form dense thickets that provide critical habitat for a myriad of species. Their submerged roots offer refuge for juvenile fish and crustaceans, while their branches serve as nesting sites for numerous bird species.

Beyond their ecological importance, mangroves play a crucial role in maintaining water quality. Their intricate root systems filter pollutants and trap sediments, contributing to the clarity of the surrounding waters. Furthermore, they act as natural buffers against storm surges, safeguarding the coastline from erosion and flooding.

**Submerged Meadows the Sea grass Beds:** Beneath the surface, vast meadows of sea grass sway gently in the currents, forming the foundation of a critical marine habitat. These submerged grasslands provide food and shelter for a diverse array of organisms, from tiny invertebrates to large marine mammals. Sea grass beds serve as nurseries for many commercially valuable fish species, contributing significantly to the region's fishing industry.

The ecological significance of sea grass extends beyond its role as a habitat. These underwater meadows help stabilize sediments, preventing erosion and maintaining water clarity. They also act as carbon sinks, absorbing carbon dioxide from the atmosphere and mitigating the effects of climate change.

**Terrestrial Havens the Hardwood Hammocks:** Contrasting with the coastal and marine environments, patches of hardwood hammocks punctuate the Keys' landscape. These dense forests, dominated by broad-leaved trees like mahogany and gumbo limbo, provide refuge for a variety of terrestrial species. Birds, reptiles, and mammals, including the endangered Key deer, find shelter within these verdant havens.

Hardwood hammocks represent a unique ecosystem within the Keys, showcasing the diversity of life that thrives in this subtropical environment. They serve as a reminder of the interconnectedness of all living things, highlighting the importance of preserving these habitats for future generations.

**Conservation Imperatives Safeguarding a Fragile Paradise:** The unique ecosystem of the Florida Keys faces numerous challenges, including climate change, pollution, and habitat loss. Recognizing the fragility of this environment, a concerted effort is underway to protect and preserve its natural treasures.

National parks, such as Biscayne National Park and Dry Tortugas National Park, safeguard critical habitats and provide opportunities for visitors to experience the wonders of the Keys' ecosystem first hand. Wildlife refuges, like the National Key Deer

Refuge, offer sanctuary for endangered species, ensuring their continued survival.

Marine sanctuaries, such as the Florida Keys National Marine Sanctuary, protect the coral reefs and other marine habitats, promoting responsible fishing practices and regulating human activities to minimize environmental impact.

The Florida Keys stand as a testament to the intricate beauty and delicate balance of nature. Our understanding and appreciation of these ecosystems' interconnectedness can help preserve the Keys' magic for future generations.

# Chapter 1: Planning Your Trip

## The best time to visit

The Florida Keys boast a tropical climate, meaning warm weather year-round. However, certain times offer a more ideal experience depending on your priorities.

**Dry Season (November-April):**

**Pros:** This period offers the most pleasant weather with lower humidity, less rainfall, and sunshine-filled days. Temperatures average in the mid-70s°F (24°C), perfect for outdoor activities.

**Cons:** This is peak tourist season, so expect higher prices and larger crowds, especially around holidays.

**Wet Season (May-October):**

**Pros:** While there's a higher chance of rain showers (usually short-lived), the wet season offers warmer ocean temperatures, ideal for swimming and water sports. Prices tend to be lower, and crowds are thinner.

**Cons:** Humidity levels rise, and this is also hurricane season (June 1st–November 30th). It's important to be aware of potential storms and have travel insurance.

**Shoulder Seasons (April-May & September-October):**

**Pros:** These shoulder months offer a sweet spot with pleasant weather, fewer crowds, and potentially lower prices. Cons: April can see an influx of spring break crowds, while September and October fall within hurricane season.

**Unique Experiences:**

- December-February: Enjoy holiday festivities and events, including Key West's New Year's Eve "shoe drop."
- March: Experience lively spring break celebrations (mainly in Key West).
- April-May: Ideal for fishing enthusiasts, with various tournaments and excellent catches.
- June-August: Lobster mini-season (late July/early August) attracts avid divers and snorkelers.
- September-October: Witness the fascinating migration of birds through the Keys.

**Important Note:** Hurricane season is a factor to consider. While hurricanes are not an everyday occurrence, it's crucial to be prepared and stay informed about weather conditions, especially if traveling during these months.

*Ultimately, the best time to visit the Florida Keys depends on your preferences for weather, crowds, and budget.*

# Why Visit in 2025?

While the Florida Keys are always a fantastic getaway, 2025 is shaping up to be an especially exciting year to visit this tropical paradise. Here's why:

## New and Improved Attractions:

- Key West International Airport Expansion: A major expansion project at Key West International Airport is expected to be completed in 2025. This will bring enhanced facilities, improved passenger flow, and a more modern travel experience.
- Enhanced Eco-Tourism: The Keys are committed to sustainable tourism. Look for new eco-tours, initiatives focused on coral reef restoration, and expanded opportunities to experience the natural beauty of the islands responsibly.
- New and Renovated Resorts: Several new hotels and resorts are expected to open or complete renovations in 2025, offering fresh accommodation options for various budgets and preferences.

## Exciting Events and Festivals:

27th Anniversary of the Key West Half Marathon & 5k (January 18-19, 2025): This popular event will be extra special as it celebrates its 27th anniversary. Runners and spectators alike can enjoy the race and the accompanying festivities, including the Papa's Pilar Rum Stroll and Key West Beach N' Beer Mile.

Potential New Events: Keep an eye out for announcements about new festivals and events planned for 2025. The Keys are known for their lively celebrations, and there's always something new happening.

## Anniversary Celebrations:

Key West's 200th Anniversary (March 25, 2025): Key West will be commemorating its bicentennial in 2025! Expect special events, historical exhibits, and celebrations throughout the year to mark this significant milestone.

## Beyond the Usual:

- Unique Art Exhibitions: The vibrant arts scene in the Keys is constantly evolving. 2025 will likely bring fresh exhibitions and installations to galleries and museums throughout the islands.
- Culinary Delights: The Keys' food scene is always innovating. Look for new restaurant openings, innovative culinary experiences, and exciting food festivals showcasing the freshest local seafood and flavors.

With new developments, exciting events, and a focus on sustainability, 2025 promises to be a memorable year to experience the unique charm and beauty of the Florida Keys.

# Getting There & Around

With a variety of transportation choices, getting to the Florida Keys and touring the islands is simple.

**Air Travel:**

- The nearest major airport, Miami International Airport (MIA), has a multitude of domestic and international connections for those wishing to reach the Keys. To get to the Keys from MIA, hire a vehicle or use a shuttle.
- For those traveling directly to Key West, Key West International Airport (EYW) is a handy choice since it provides direct flights from many American cities.

**Driving:**

Overseas Highway (US 1): This picturesque route, which links the Keys to Florida's mainland, provides breath taking vistas of the ocean and an unforgettable road trip experience. Be advised that traffic, particularly during the busiest seasons of the year, might cause delays in travel times.

**Ferry services:**

Key West Express: A leisurely substitute for driving, this high-speed boat service connects Fort Myers Beach and Marco Island to Key West.

**Traveling Around the Keys:**

- Rental cars provide you the freedom to go at your own speed. But in certain places, parking may be costly and scarce.
- In Key West and other densely populated places, taxis are easily accessible.
- Public Transportation: In Key West, reasonably priced transportation is available via the Key West Transit bus system.
- Renting a bicycle is a well-liked and environmentally responsible method to get about, particularly in Key West and Islamorada.
- Boat tours and water taxis provide access to isolated locations and islands as well as distinctive views of the Keys.

**Advice for Travel:**

- Plan ahead for boat tickets and auto rentals, particularly during busy times.
- Because of the considerable distances between islands, travel times should be taken into account while organizing events.
- To prevent parking problems in congested locations, take the bus or ride your bike.
- Take into account boat cruises or private charters if you want to go to remote islands or explore the hinterland.

Accessing and navigating the Florida Keys is easy because of the many transportation alternatives available, which also let you customize your trip to your liking.

# Visa & Entry

Make sure you have the required paperwork for admission into the United States before starting your Florida Keys tour. This is a brief guide on international traveler visa requirements:

**Program for Visa Waiver (VWP):**

Countries That Qualify: Under the VWP, citizens of 40 countries—including the majority of European countries, Australia, New Zealand, Japan, and South Korea—may be able to enter the United States for up to 90 days for business or pleasure without a visa.

ESTA prerequisite: You still need to get an online clearance for the Electronic System for Travel Authorization (ESTA) before your travel, even if you are eligible for the VWP. At least 72 hours before departure, submit an ESTA application.

*Important Information: Only passengers arriving by air or sea are covered by the VWP.*

**Non-Immigrant Visa:**

- Required for: Visitors from non-VWP member nations or those intending to remain for more than ninety days will need a non-immigrant visa.
- Application Procedure: Visit a U.S. embassy or consulate in your nation of residence to submit an application for a visa. Make plans appropriately since the procedure might take weeks or months.

## Essential Documentation:

- Valid Passport: Your passport must remain valid for at least six months after the length of time you want to spend in the United States.
- Return Ticket: To prove that you intend to depart the United States, provide documentation of a return or onward ticket.
- Financial Sufficiency: Be ready to provide proof that you have enough money to pay for all of your costs while there.

**Particular Rules for 2025:** Remain Current: Rules and policies pertaining to visas are subject to change. For the most recent information prior to your travel in 2025, check the U.S. Department of State's official website or speak with the U.S. embassy or consulate in your area.

## Important Remainders:

- Processing Times for Visas: The length of time it takes to process a visa varies based on the season and your country. To prevent delays, apply much in advance.
- Travel Insurance: Getting travel insurance that covers medical crises, trip cancellations, and other unanticipated events is strongly advised.

You may guarantee a hassle-free and seamless start to your 2025 Florida Keys vacation by being aware of these visa and entrance procedures.

## Essential Tips

Here are some helpful hints to help you get ready and guarantee a hassle-free, pleasurable Florida Keys vacation:

**Essentials of Packing:**

- Dressing: Bring light attire, such as swimsuits, t-shirts, shorts, and a lightweight jacket or sweater for chilly nights. Remember to bring suitable walking shoes, sunglasses, and a hat.
- Sun Protection: The sun is fierce in Florida! To shield yourself from damaging UV rays, bring sunglasses, a wide-brimmed hat, and sunscreen with a high SPF.
- Insect Repellent: During the rainy season, mosquitoes and other insects may be present. To prevent mosquito bites, bring insect repellent.

- Essentials such as bandages, painkillers, antiseptic wipes, and any personal prescriptions should be included in a first-aid kit.
- Additional necessities are a compact flashlight, a reusable water bottle, a waterproof bag for valuables, and a travel adaptor if necessary.

## Exchange of currency and payments:

- The US dollar: The U.S. dollar (USD) is the currency used in the Florida Keys.
- Credit Cards: Most people take credit cards. To prevent any problems with card use, let your bank know when you will be traveling.
- ATMs: For cash withdrawals, ATMs are easily accessible across the Keys.
- Currency swap: If necessary, swap money at currency exchange offices in major cities or before your journey.

## Tipping Customs:

- For excellent service, restaurants often tip 15% to 20% of the pre-tax total.
- Bars: 15-20% of the bill or $1-2 per drink.
- 15–25% of the fee goes to the taxi drivers.
- Bellhops: one to two bags.
- Daily housekeeping costs: $2–5.

## Keeping Safe:

- 911 is the emergency number for any situation (police, fire, ambulance).
- Healthcare: The Keys are home to hospitals and clinics. It is strongly advised to get travel insurance.
- Water Safety: Observe any flags and warning signs that are shown at beaches. Watch out for aquatic creatures and strong currents.
- Sun Safety: During the warmest hours of the day, seek shade, use sunscreen, and drink plenty of water.
- Hurricane Season: Be aware of the weather and have a plan in case of a storm if you are traveling between June 1st and November 30th.

**Conscientious Travel:**

- Honor the Environment Stay on designated paths, dispose of waste appropriately, and stay away from single-use plastics.
- Preserve marine life by avoiding the use of dangerous sunscreen chemicals and by not touching or disturbing coral reefs.
- Support Local Businesses: To help the community's economy, patronize nearby eateries, retail establishments, and tour companies.
- Respect Local Culture: Pay attention to local traditions and noise levels.

You may guarantee a responsible, fun, and safe vacation to the Florida Keys while also having a beneficial effect on the local community and environment by adhering to these guidelines.

# Chapter 2: 14-Day Itinerary

### Days 1-3: Key Largo: Dive into Paradise

- Explore John Penne-kamp Coral Reef State Park, snorkel, or dive amidst vibrant coral reefs.
- Kayak through mangrove forests and encounter diverse marine life.
- Relax on pristine beaches and savor fresh seafood at waterfront restaurants.

### Days 4-6: Islamorada—Cast Your Line and Embrace Island Life

- Embark on a thrilling sport-fishing charter and reel in a trophy catch.
- Witness playful dolphins at theater of the Sea.
- Explore the local artist scene and find one-of-a-kind treasures.
- Indulge in fresh seafood feasts and enjoy waterfront dining with breath-taking sunsets.

# Days 7-9: Marathon—Bridge the Gap between Adventure and Relaxation

- Drive across the iconic Seven Mile Bridge, marveling at engineering ingenuity.
- Learn about marine conservation at the Turtle Hospital and encounter rescued sea turtles.
- Explore the historic Pigeon Key and uncover its fascinating past.
- Enjoy family-friendly activities and relax on beautiful beaches.

# Days 10-12: Big Pine Key & the Lower Keys— Unplug and Unwind

- Venture into the National Key Deer Refuge and spot the adorable miniature Key deer.
- Discover secluded beaches and hidden coves perfect for kayaking and paddle boarding.
- Unplug from the hustle and bustle and embrace the tranquil island life.
- Savor delicious key lime pie and local seafood at charming eateries.

# Days 13-14: Key West—Soak Up the Sun and the Quirky Vibes

- Immerse yourself in the vibrant atmosphere of Key West.

- Visit Ernest Hemingway's house and learn about the legendary author.
- Stroll down Duval Street, soaking up the lively energy and unique shops.
- Celebrate the sunset at Mallory Square with street performers and fellow travelers.
- Explore historical landmarks and embrace the island's quirky charm.

# Chapter 3: Key Largo

## Top Attractions

Adventurers and nature lovers will find paradise on Key Largo, the first island in the Florida Keys archipelago. As the "Dive Capital of the World," it is well-known for its colorful coral reefs, verdant hammocks, and intriguing past. The following must-see sights encapsulate Key Largo's spirit:

**Pennekamp, John Coral Reef State Park:** This underwater paradise, which protected a 70-nautical-square-mile section of the Florida Reef Tract, was the country's first underwater park.

- Explore the Depths: Discover thriving coral reefs that are brimming with aquatic life. Amidst vibrant fish, sea turtles, and sometimes even reef sharks, go snorkeling or scuba diving.
- Glass-Bottom Boat Trips: These trips provide a glimpse of this underwater environment for those who would rather remain dry.
- Kayaking and canoeing: Explore the mangrove paths while taking in the distinctive habitat and a variety of birds.
- Hiking paths: Take small nature paths that meander through tropical hammocks to see the park's natural splendor.

**Realistic Specifics:**

- Open every day of the year from 8:00 AM until dusk.
- $8 per car (plus 50 cents per passenger) is the fee.

- Accessibility: Facilities and trails are wheelchair accessible.

**Dagny Johnson Key Largo Hammock Botanical State Park:** Johnson, Dagny One of the biggest areas of West Indian tropical hardwood hammock in the US is preserved at Key Largo Hammock Botanical State Park.

- Bird-watching Paradise: The varied ecosystems attract a large range of bird species, making it a refuge for birdwatchers.
- Nature Trails: Trek or ride a bike over six miles of trails, where you may come across uncommon flora and creatures, including wild cotton, mahogany mistletoe, and the American crocodile.
- Possibilities for Photography: Take in the splendor of the varied fauna, distinctive flora, and lush greenery.

**Realistic Specifics:**

- Open every day of the year from 8:00 AM until dusk.
- Fees: honor system, $2.50 per person.
- Accessibility: Some paths are not wheelchair accessible.

**The African Queen:** Take a ride on this famous riverboat, which was featured in the 1951 movie starring Katharine Hepburn and Humphrey Bogart.

- Historical Boat Tours: participate in guided boat tours through the Port Largo Canals and discover the history of the vessel and the region's distinctive ecology.
- Sunset Cruises: From the deck of this ancient ship, take in the splendor of a Key Largo sunset.
- Private Charters: For special events or small parties, the African Queen is also available for private charter.

**Practical Information: Hours: Depending on the trip, they may vary.**

- The cost varies based on the trip.
- Accessibility: Because the boat is historic, it is not easily accessible.

**Beyond the Basics:**

- Visit Key Largo Undersea Park to see marine life from an underwater observation platform and immerse yourself in an underwater ecosystem.
- Visit the Florida Keys Wild Bird Rehabilitation Center to observe a variety of species up close and learn about the rescue and rehabilitation of wounded birds.
- Key Largo Conch House: This unusual house in the style of a conch shell is a wonderful place to get local crafts, artwork, and souvenirs.

Explore these sites and wander off the usual routes to discover the variety of experiences that make Key Largo such an enthralling place.

# Dining & Cuisine

With a variety of alternatives to suit every taste and price range, Key Largo's eating scene is as varied as its underwater scenery. A little peek at what's to come:

**Waterfront Gems & Casual Bites:**

The Fish House: This Key Largo landmark offers deliciously fresh fish in a relaxed setting. Their "hook-and-cook" option lets you bring in your catch and cook it. (MM 102.5 | $$$ | Views of the waterfront, outdoor seats)

Sundowners: Savor delectable seafood and tropical beverages at this waterfront restaurant while taking in the stunning sunset views. Locals love its conch fritters and lobster bisque. (MM 104 | $$$ | Live music, waterfront dining)

A staple of Key Largo, Mrs. Mac's Kitchen is renowned for its Key lime pie, home-style cuisine, and hearty quantities. Don't pass up their renowned Reuben sandwich with lobster. (MM 99.4 | $$ | Family-friendly, informal)

Key Largo Conch House: This unusual eatery, which is fashioned like a huge conch shell, has a laid-back vibe and serves Key lime pie, conch fritters, and fresh seafood. (MM 100.2 | $$ | Distinct ambiance, alfresco seats)

## Luxurious Dining & Global Tastes:

Sol by the Sea: Savor a classy meal at a premium restaurant with breath-taking views of the ocean. They provide creative seafood dishes and fresh, locally produced ingredients on their menu. (MM 100 | $$$$ | romantic atmosphere, waterfront eating) The Grove Kitchen & Bar: In a chic environment, savor delectable American cuisine with an emphasis on seasonal, fresh ingredients. They have inventive delicacies like grilled octopus and pan-seared scallops on their menu. (MM 99.7 | $$$ | Craft drinks, modern atmosphere)

In a stunning waterfront location, savor delicious seafood with Caribbean flavors at Snapper's Waterfront Restaurant. You should definitely try their grilled mahi-mahi and conch soup. (MM 94.5 | $$$ | Live music, waterfront dining)

## Important Lime Pie and Regional Specialties:

Key Lime Pie: Enjoying this famous delicacy is a must when visiting Key Largo. Try it at any of the neighborhood bakeries, The Fish House, or Mrs. Mac's Kitchen.

Key Largo's signature dish is conch fritters, which are flavorful and crunchy. You may find them in most eateries, such as Key Largo Conch House and The Fish House.

Fresh Seafood: Key Largo is a haven for seafood enthusiasts. Most restaurants provide fresh seafood, including lobster, mahi-mahi, grouper, and snapper.

**Beyond the Basics:**

- Food Trucks: Taste the variety of food trucks in Key Largo, which serve anything from Cuban sandwiches and smoothies to tacos and burgers.
- Farmers Markets: Visit the Key Largo Farmers Market to get locally grown veggies, honey, and other handcrafted items.
- Cooking workshops: Some resorts and culinary schools provide practical cooking workshops where guests may learn how to make delectable Key Largo dishes.

Key Largo provides a delectable experience for every taste and price range thanks to its varied culinary scene. You're likely to find something to sate your hunger, whether it's casual seafood, fine dining, or the famous Key lime pie.

## Accommodations

Whether you're looking for opulent beachfront resorts, family-friendly getaways, or affordable retreats, Key Largo has a wide variety of lodging options to meet the requirements and tastes of every visitor. The following list of accommodations will help you have a relaxing and enjoyable time in the Dive Capital of the World:

**Waterfront getaways and luxury resorts:**

Autograph Collection at Playa Largo Resort & Spa: (MM 97.5 | $$$$) A private beach, several pools, a full-service spa, and river front dining are just a few of the opulent features that this sophisticated resort offers. Bungalows, suites, large guest rooms, and even private villas with plunge pools are available.

(MM 97 | $$$$) Baker's Cay Resort Key Largo, Curio Collection by Hilton At this chic resort with two pools, a private beach, beautiful gardens, and a range of water activities, you can embrace a tropical paradise. Modern conveniences and balconies with breath-taking views are features of the guest rooms and suites.

**Family-Friendly Havens:**

Key Largo Bay Marriott Beach Resort (MM 103.8 | $$$) is a family-friendly destination. Spacious rooms, a private beach, several pools (including a children's pool), and a range of activities for all ages are all features of this family-friendly resort. Savor casual surroundings, water sport rentals, and on-site restaurants.

(MM 100 | $$$) Marina Del Mar Resort & Marina This resort offers large villas with separate living rooms and fully equipped kitchens that are ideal for families. Take advantage of a playground for the kids, a marina where you can hire boats, and a private beach.

**Cozy Bed & Breakfasts:**

Bay Harbor Lodge: (MM 104 | $$) with a private dock, verdant grounds, and a laid-back vibe, this little bed and breakfast provides a peaceful haven. Savor individualized attention, cozy accommodations, and a delectable meal every morning.

(MM 97.8 | $$$) Kona Kai Resort, Gallery, and Botanic Gardens Art, nature, and leisure are all combined in this adults-only haven. Relax in the peaceful grounds, see the on-site art museum, and stay in rooms with distinctive décor.

**Private Retreats & Vacation Rentals:** Rentals for Vacations: A variety of vacation rentals are available in Key Largo, ranging from large beachfront houses to comfortable cottages. Savor the independence and seclusion that come with owning a place of your own, often complete with outside spaces, kitchens, and swimming pools. (Prices vary.)

**Low-Cost Accommodations and Campsites:** Key Largo Marina & Campground: (MM 101.5 | $) this campsite has a range of accommodations, including cabins, RV hookups, and tent sites. Take advantage of a marina with boat rentals, a swimming pool, and a beachfront setting.

Coral Reef State Park at John Pennekamp: (MM 102.5 | $) Camp at the state park under the stars for a very unique experience. Either basic tent sites or campsites with power and water connections are available.

# Nightlife

Although Key Largo is well known for its daytime activities and underwater experiences, the island also has a laid-back and welcoming nocturnal culture. After the sun sets, Key Largo has much to offer, whether you're looking for live music, views of the waterfront, or just somewhere to relax with a tropical drink.

**Live Music at Relaxed Bars:**

Caribbean Club: (MM 104) Featured in the iconic movie "Key Largo," this antique tavern embodies the charm of vintage Florida. Enjoy live music on the waterfront stage while sipping a Key Lime Pie Rum Punch. With its laid-back vibe and breath-taking sunset views, the Caribbean Club is a favorite among both residents and tourists.

Snappers Oceanfront Restaurant & Bar (MM 100) with your toes on the sand, take in live music at Snappers. This club along the seaside has a wonderful vibe and hosts local musicians who play anything from reggae to classic rock. The ideal complement to the tropical atmosphere is their famous Snappers Tropical Martini.

**Lounges by the Water and Calm Environments:**

Sundowners: (MM 104) Sundowners is the ideal spot to view the sunset over the Gulf of Mexico, as the name implies. Live music, a varied drink menu, and breath-taking views are all features of this laid-back waterfront restaurant and pub.

The Big Chill by Jimmy Johnson: (MM 104) Former NFL coach Jimmy Johnson owns this relaxed pub, which has a large assortment of specialty beers and drinks, outdoor seating, live music, and a laid-back vibe. It's a wonderful spot to relax and take in the island air.

Pilot House Restaurant & Marina (MM 100) Pilot House, tucked away in a harbor, provides a peaceful environment with views of the coastline. Enjoy a laid-back supper outside or sip on a tropical beverage while seeing the boats arrive and go.

**Outside the Bars:**

- Observing the Stars: Key Largo provides great astronomy chances with less light pollution. See the stars in a park or on a remote beach.
- Kayaking at night: Take a guided kayak journey to discover the mangroves' enchantment at night. Take in the peace and quiet of the moonlit sea while seeing nocturnal animals.

The nightlife scene in Key Largo is all about enjoying the laid-back atmosphere of the island. In this tropical paradise, you'll discover the ideal location to have a fantastic evening, whether your goals are live music, views of the waterfront, or just a place to relax with a refreshing drink.

# Water Activities

Water lovers will find heaven in Key Largo's pristine seas and varied marine environments. This underwater paradise awaits you for an aquatic adventure, regardless of your level of expertise diving or snorkeling.

**Snorkeling and Scuba Diving:**

Molasses Reef: A popular diving and snorkeling destination, this reef is located inside John Pennekamp Coral Reef State Park. Discover vivid coral formations, swim with colorful fish, and come across amazing animals like moray eels and marine turtles.

*Insider Tip: Reserve a snorkeling or diving excursion with a trustworthy company that places a high priority on reef preservation.*

The Abyss Christ: Divers and snorkelers must view this famous underwater statue, which is also in the park. A healthy reef environment surrounds the 9-foot bronze monument, which is submerged in 25 feet of water.

*Insider Tip: For a more peaceful experience, try going early in the morning or during the off-season since the monument may become busy.*

Other Dive Sites: There are a lot of other dive sites in Key Largo, such as the French Reef, the Elbow, and the Spiegel Grove shipwreck, which is an advanced dive.

*Insider Tip: Based on your interests and degree of expertise, ask local dive shops for suggestions.*

Through mangrove kayaking, discover the ecosystem: Observe the distinctive plants and animals that flourish in the complex system of mangrove forests as you paddle through them.

*Insider Tip: To understand the significance of mangroves and the animals that inhabit there, take a guided kayak excursion.*

Popular Locations: Dagny Johnson and John Pennekamp Coral Reef State Park Kayaking chances are excellent in Key Largo Hammock Botanical State Park.

*Insider Tip: Keep an eye out for fish, crabs, birds, and sometimes even crocodiles or manatees!*

Offshore Adventures: Fishing Charters: Take a deep-sea fishing charter and play for marlin, sailfish, tuna, and other valuable game fish.

*Insider Tip: Reserve a charter with a seasoned skipper who is familiar with the top fishing locations.*

Backcountry Fishing: Investigate Florida Bay's shallow areas and hunt permits, tarpon, and bonefish.

*Insider Tip: For a more personalized experience, choose a guide with expertise in wilderness fishing.*

Sunset Cruises: Romantic Getaways: Take your significant other on a romantic sunset cruise while drinking champagne and admiring the vibrantly colored sky.

*Insider Tip: For a more personal experience, book a private charter.*

Family Fun: participate in a sunset cruise that has live entertainment and music, making it the ideal family adventure.

*Insider Tip: Although many sunset cruises include beverages and snacks, you may wish to pack your own.*

Avoid touching coral, use sunscreen that is safe for reefs, and dispose of waste correctly to show your respect for the marine environment.

# Chapter 4: Islamorada

## Top Attractions

Known as the Sport-fishing Capital of the World," Islamorada combines breath-taking scenery, exhilarating experiences, and a relaxed island atmosphere. Here are a few must-see sights that perfectly encapsulate this fascinating the key

**Theater of the Sea:**

- This marine mamals park offers a unique chance to get up close and personal with sea lions, dolphins, and other aquatic animals.
- Dolphin shows: Discover the behavior and communication of these clever creatures while seeing them pull off amazing feats.

- Sea Lion Encounters: Learn about the distinct personalities and characteristics of playful sea lions up close.
- Additional Activities: The park provides a range of additional activities, such as glass-bottom boat tours, swimming with dolphins, and snorkeling with sea lions.

**Realistic Specifics:**

- Daily hours are 9:30 AM to 4:00 PM.
- Entry fees: Adult general entry begins at $42.95.
- Accessibility: The majority of the park is wheelchair accessible.

**Robbie's Marina:** This busy marina is a terrific spot to feel the local vibe and is a centre for water sports. Watch as enormous tarpon jump out of the water to grab fish out of your fingers while they feed.

*Insider Tip: If you want to see the tarpon feeding frenzy, go there early in the morning or late in the afternoon.*

Kayaking and paddle boarding: Take a kayak or paddleboard rental and explore the surrounding waterways and the mangrove-lined creeks.

*Insider Tip: As you paddle around the placid waters, keep an eye out for manatees, dolphins, and a variety of bird species.*

Additional Activities: Robbie's also provides sunset cruises, snorkeling excursions, and fishing charters.

**Practical Information:**

- Hours: Change according to the activity.
- The cost varies based on the activity.
- Accessibility: Wheelchair users may often reach the mariana and its environs.

**The Diving Museum's History:** Explore the intriguing past of underwater research at this one-of-a-kind museum.

- Exhibits: Learn about the development of diving gear, from the first diving bells to the most recent scuba gear.
- Discover a variety of items, such as vintage diving helmets, underwater cameras, and objects found in shipwrecks.
- Programs for Education: For people of all ages, the museum provides educational activities and programs.

**Practical Information:**

- Daily hours are 10:00 AM to 5:00 PM.
- The adult fee is $14.
- Accessibility: Wheelchair users may enter the museum.

You'll have a greater understanding of Islamorada's distinctive fusion of historical importance, marine life encounters, and natural beauty by investigating these attractions.

# Dining & Cuisine

With a variety of eateries that turn fresh fish into mouth-watering meals, Islamorada's culinary scene is a celebration of the sea. Every seafood lover's cravings will be met by Islamorada's varied selection, whether they are for a laid-back beachside lunch or an elegant fine dining experience.

**Dining by the Water with sweeping views:**

Beach Cafe at Morada Bay: (MM 81.6 | $$) with stunning views of the Atlantic Ocean, this beachside haven provides a dining experience that is right on the beach. Savor locally sourced, fresh seafood in a laid-back setting with live music. The Morada Bay Seafood Platter, which has a variety of the day's finest catches, and Grilled Mahi-Mahi with mango salsa are two of their specialties.

(MM 83 | $$$) Ziggie & Mad Dog's Oceanside Restaurant This iconic Islamorada restaurant has a vibrant environment, expansive views of the ocean, and seafood specialties with a Caribbean flair. Savor their "World Famous" Lobster Reuben, Jerk-Spiced Mahi-Mahi, or Conch Chowder. In addition, Ziggie & Mad Dog's offers tropical drinks and a large wine selection.

**Casual Dining Establishments with an Island Feel:**

(MM 83 | $$) Wahoo's Bar & Grill With live music and a cuisine that features fresh seafood and regional specialties, this laid-back waterfront restaurant provides a relaxed environment. Savor the tropical atmosphere while indulging in their well-known Fish Tacos, Conch Fritters, and Key Lime Pie.

The Tarpon in Hunger: (MM 77.5 | $$) this relaxed eatery in Robbie's Marina provides a distinctive dining experience. Savor sandwiches, burgers, and fresh seafood while watching the tarpon feeding frenzy. Don't pass up the chance to hand-feed the enormous tarpon and their renowned lobster roll.

**Elegant Eating & Creative Cooking:**

Casa Morada: (MM 81.6 | $$$$) The fine dining restaurant at this small, adults-only resort specializes in creative cooking using local, fresh ingredients. Seared scallops with truffle sauce and grilled swordfish with citrus blanc are two of their creatively prepared menu items. Savor a romantic meal while admiring breath-taking views of the ocean.

(MM 81.7 | $$$$) The Square Grouper Bar & Grill Fresh, sustainably farmed fish is the main attraction at this elegant restaurant. They have inventive delicacies like lobster ravioli with truffle cream sauce and pan-seared yellowtail snapper with mango salsa on their menu. The Square Grouper also serves handmade cocktails and has a large wine selection.

**Beyond the Plate:**

Islamorada Fish Company: (MM 81.5) a range of fresh catches are available for purchase or consumption on-site at this well-known seafood market and restaurant. Fish & Chips, Fried Shrimp, and Conch Chowder are among the traditional meals served at their laid-back restaurant.

Brewing Company of the Florida Keys: (MM 81.6) This Islamorada brewery offers locally crafted beers to go with your seafood feast. Savor a pint of their signature Islamorada Ale or partake in a taster flight.

Discover the authentic tastes of Islamorada by sampling these varied eating alternatives, where inventive cooking and fresh seafood come together to create a wonderful dining experience.

## Accommodations

A wide variety of lodging options are available in Islamorada to accommodate every traveler's preferences and price range. After a day of touring this island paradise, you'll find the ideal spot to relax, whether you're looking for an opulent beachside hideaway, a quaint boutique hotel, or a comfortable guesthouse.

**Top-Notch Resorts:**

Lodge & Spa Cheeca: (MM 82 | $$$$) Situated on 27 acres of beachfront land, this renowned resort has a rich history, opulent facilities, and a fantastic position. Savor championship golf, a world-class spa, several pools, and a private beach. Private villas, bungalows, suites, and tasteful guest rooms are available.

MM 80.2 | $$$ La Siesta Resort & Marina With a private beach, several pools, a marina, and a range of water activities, this family-friendly resort has a laid-back vibe. Choose from villas with fully equipped kitchens, suites, or roomy guest rooms.

**Boutique Hotels with a Touch of the Islands:**

The Village of Moorings: (MM 81.6 | $$$$) this remote hideaway has a number of individual cottages surrounded by beautiful tropical vegetation. Savor the peace and quiet, a freshwater pool, and a secluded beach. The Moorings Village is a well-liked destination for calm escapes and romantic retreats.

Resort Amara Cay: (MM 80 | $$) with an emphasis on rest and renewal, this chic resort has a modern style. Savor a rooftop bar with breath-taking views of the ocean, a private beach, and an infinity pool. Amara Cay combines tropical beauty with contemporary conveniences.

**Charming Guesthouses & Inns:**

The Chesapeake Beach Resort has charming guesthouses and inns (MM 82 | $$). This family-run resort has a private beach, a pool, and a range of water activities in a laid-back setting. Select from cozy apartments, cottages with kitchenettes, or guest rooms.

Villas on the Island: (MM 82.1 | $$$) with a private beach, a pool, and beautiful tropical plants, this small group of villas provides a peaceful haven. Savor roomy lodgings with private balconies and fully equipped kitchens.

**Rentals for all types of vacations:**

- Villas by the Sea: Savor the luxury of a private seaside home with breathtaking views, roomy quarters, and exclusive features like hot tubs and pools. (Prices vary.)
- Family-Friendly Homes: Look for roomy vacation rentals that are ideal for gatherings of friends or family, with private pools, complete kitchens, and many bedrooms. (Prices vary.)
- Budget-Friendly Cottages: Find quaint cottages and bungalows that provide a comfortable and reasonably priced haven. (Prices vary.)

Islamorada provides friendly lodging to guarantee a relaxing and unforgettable stay on this island paradise, regardless of your preferences or price range.

# Nightlife

Islamorada offers a more laid-back and private ambiance at night, while its days are full of sunlight and water sports. Islamorada's nightlife scene has something for everyone, whether you're looking for a romantic evening beneath the stars, a laid-back venue to hang out with friends, or live music with views of the ocean.

**Live music while you observe:**

Cabana Bar & Lorelei Restaurant: (MM 82) This Islamorada landmark is well known for its vibrant ambiance and breath-taking views of Florida Bay at sunset. Take in live music every night, with local bands performing a variety of rock, reggae, and tropical songs. Enjoy a specialty drink, such as the Pain Killer or the Rum Runner, while taking in the atmosphere of the island.

Morada Bay Beach Cafe (MM 81.6) with your toes in the sand, this beachside haven provides a distinctive atmosphere for taking in live music. Local musicians play a range of styles, including reggae, island rhythms, and acoustic guitar. Sip a tropical cocktail, relax in a beach chair, and let the music take you back to the island.

**Waterfront bars and informal get-togethers:**

Marker 88: (MM 88) with expansive views of the ocean, this Islamorada mainstay provides a vibrant environment. Savor casual cuisine with fresh seafood and regional specialties, live music on certain evenings, and happy hour deals. A wonderful spot to get together with friends and take in the relaxed atmosphere of the island is Marker 88.

Wahoo's Bar & Grill (MM 83) this beachfront restaurant has a laid-back vibe, live music, and a welcoming ambiance. Savor a relaxed lunch, a refreshing beverage, and a variety of local artists performing. Wahoo's a well-liked destination for both residents and tourists.

(MM 85.3) Hog Heaven Sports Bar Consider going to Hog Heaven if you want a livelier setting. This well-known sports pub has late-night food, live music, and many TVs in a relaxed atmosphere. It's a terrific spot to meet other tourists, have a refreshing drink, and watch a game.

**Quiet Evenings and Romantic Escapes:**

Pierre's Restaurant (MM 81.6) on some evenings, this classy waterfront restaurant has live piano music in a refined setting. Savor a romantic supper in a classy setting while taking in breath-taking views of the ocean.

Morada Casa: (MM 81.6) for a romantic evening, this small, adults-only resort provides a peaceful environment. Savor a delectable dinner at their well-known restaurant, relax by the pool, or have a beverage at their waterfront bar.

**Outside the Bars:**

- Stargazing: Get away from the lights and visit a remote park or beach to take in the night sky's constellations. Islamorada is a wonderful place to see stars because it has low levels of light pollution.
- Night Kayaking: Take a guided kayak journey to discover the mangroves' enchantment at night. Take in the peace and quiet of the moonlit sea while seeing nocturnal animals.

Whatever your taste, Islamorada's nightlife scene provides a laid-back and welcoming setting where you can relax, make new friends, and enjoy the island's easy going vibe.

# Water Activities

The "Sport-fishing Capital of the World" moniker is well-earned, but Islamorada has much more to offer in the water than just a line. Islamorada's variety of water-sports will leave you wanting more, whether your preference is for peaceful paddles through mangroves, exhilarating undersea explorations, or island-hopping excursions.

**Charters for Sport Fishing:**

Trophy Fish Target: Prized game species like marlin, sailfish, tuna, mahi-mahi, and wahoo are abundant in Islamorada's seas. To pursue your prize catch, charter a boat with a skilled captain and crew to traverse the Gulf Stream and offshore reefs.

*Insider Tip: Fly fishing, light tackle, and deep-sea fishing are among the half-day or full-day excursions that several charters provide.*

Wilderness fishing: For a unique fishing experience, go into the shallow waters of Florida Bay and the wilderness of Everglades National Park. In these pristine habitats, target species such as redfish, permit, tarpon, and bonefish.

*Insider Tip: To negotiate the shallow waters and provide knowledgeable guidance, hire a guide with experience in wilderness fishing.*

**Diving and snorkeling adventures:**

Examine coral reefs: Explore the Florida Keys National Marine Sanctuary's colorful underwater environment. At well-known reefs like Alligator Reef, Cheeca Rocks, and Davis Reef, you may dive or snorkel and see a variety of marine life, including sea turtles and vibrant fish.

*Insider Tip: For a safer and more educational experience, choose a guided diving or snorkeling excursion.*

Shipwreck Dives: Islamorada provides chances for seasoned divers to investigate intriguing shipwrecks, such as the Eagle and the Spiegel Grove.

*Insider Tip: Make sure you possess the training and credentials required for shipwreck diving.*

**Paddle-boarding and kayaking:**

Calm Paddles: Take a kayak or paddleboard ride around Florida Bay's serene waters and mangrove-lined waterways. See a variety of birds, get up close and personal with marine life such as dolphins and manatees, and take in the tranquility of nature.

*Insider Tip: Robbie's Marina and other nearby outfitters rent out kayaks and paddleboards.*

Guided Tours: For a more educational experience, sign up for a guided kayak or paddleboard tour. Discover undiscovered coves, gain understanding of nature, and have fun with an informed guide.

*Insider Tip: For a really spectacular experience, think about going for a sunset paddle.*

**Boat Cruises to Adjacent Islands:**

Island Hopping: Take a boat cruise to see neighboring islands such as Lignumvitae Key Botanical State Park, Indian Key Historic State Park, or the quiet Lower Keys beaches.

*Insider Tip: A lot of boat trips include possibilities for swimming, beachcombing, and snorkeling.*

Sunset Cruises: Savor a romantic sunset cruise while seeing the Florida Keys and the sky's brilliant hues.

*Insider Tip: For a more individualized and exclusive experience, book a private charter.*

Islamorada has many options for exploration and adventure due to its plethora of water-based activities. This island paradise offers the ideal aquatic experience, whether you're looking for excitement or peace.

# Chapter 5: Marathon

## Top Attractions

**Marathon unveiling the Middle Keys' Hidden Gems:** Located in the centre of the Florida Keys, Marathon provides an enthralling fusion of historical intrigue, natural beauty, and aquatic experiences. With a wide variety of things to suit everyone's interests, this island paradise begs for exploration.

Marine Life Encounters: The Turtle Hospital (MM 48.5) See the commitment and kindness of this well-known sea turtle rehabilitation facility. Educational tours provide visitors with a better understanding of the hospital's goals, the difficulties these endangered animals confront, and the incredible recovery stories of its patients.

- Tours are offered every day from 9:00 AM to 3:00 PM.

- Adult admission is $25; children's entry is $12.
- Accessibility: Suitable for wheelchair users.

Dolphin Research Centre (MM 59) Visit this non-profit research and education centre to get a first-hand look at dolphins. While observation areas provide a peek of these sophisticated animals' normal habits, interactive programs give visitors the chance to interact with them.

- Daily operating hours are 9:00 AM to 4:30 PM; significant holidays are closed.
- Adult admission is $28; children's admission is $23.
- Accessibility: Suitable for wheelchair users.

Crane Point Museum & Nature Centre: (MM 50.5) Examining History and Nature At this 63-acre preserve, take a trip through the Florida Keys' natural and historical fabric. Discover the rich history of the area at the on-site museum, go through a variety of habitats, and come across local plants and animals.

- Daily operating hours are 9:00 AM to 5:00 PM.
- Adult admission is $15; children's entry is $8.
- Accessibility: Wheelchair users may visit the museum and some of the paths.

Famous landmarks and breath-taking views include the Seven Mile Bridge (MM 40–47). Explore this famous monument, an engineering wonder that links the Lower Keys and Marathon. As you cross this ancient bridge, take in the breath-taking panoramic vistas of the Atlantic Ocean and the Gulf of Mexico.

**Accessibility:** Open to cars, pedestrians, and bikes twenty-four hours a day. Pigeon Key offers parking for those who want to explore the Old Seven Mile Bridge.

### Beyond the Highlights

Sombrero Beach (MM 50): Unwind on the immaculate sands of this well-liked beach, which is well-known for its serene waves and welcoming environment for families. Take pleasure in beachcombing, swimming, picnicking, and tanning.

Curry Hammock State Park (MM 56.2) Find a sanctuary for outdoor exploration, kayaking, and paddle-boarding. Experience the peace and quiet of this seaside paradise while paddling along mangrove pathways and taking in the varied birds.

Every tourist to Marathon is guaranteed an engaging and remarkable experience because of its many attractions and intriguing fusion of history, nature, and marine experiences.

## Dining & Cuisine

With a gastronomic journey that includes fresh seafood, waterfront vistas, and cosmopolitan cuisines, Marathon's eating scene is as varied as its attractions. Marathon's restaurants are likely to please any pallet, whether you're looking for a laid-back beachside lunch, a romantic evening with a sunset background, or a taste of international cuisine.

**New Catches with Views of the Ocean:**

Keys Marina & Fisheries Market: (MM 49) with breath-taking views of the Gulf of Mexico, this beachfront jewel provides a laid-back vibe. As you watch the fishing boats arrive and go, savor fresh seafood straight from the boat, including their well-known lobster reuben. A range of fresh fish are available in their market for you to cook at home.

Southern Lazy Days: (MM 50.5) Savor delicious seafood with a touch of the Caribbean while unwinding on their large veranda with a view of the ocean. Local specialties including grilled mahi-mahi, smoked fish dip, and conch fritters are on their menu. On certain evenings, Lazy Days South also has live music and a bustling joyful hour.

**Casual Bites and Local Flavors:**

Snacks and Regional Tastes: Porky's Bayside Barbecue & Smokehouse: (MM 47.5) Savor delectable barbecue at this laid-back restaurant with views of the harbor. Along with delectable sides and regional craft brews, their menu offers BBQ favorites like pulled pork, brisket, and smoked ribs.

Waterfront in Burdines: (MM 48.5) this family-friendly eatery has a laid-back vibe with a varied menu that includes tropical drinks, American staples, and fresh seafood. As the sun sets over the sea, savor their well-known Fish Tacos, Conch Chowder, and Key Lime Pie.

**International Food and Elegant Dining:**

Butterfly Cafe (MM 48.5) with an emphasis on world-tropical cuisine, this classy restaurant at Tranquility Bay Resort provides a sophisticated dining experience. Seared scallops with mango salsa and grilled swordfish with lemon blank are two of their creatively prepared meals made using local, fresh ingredients.

Castaway Sushi Bar & Waterfront Restaurant: (MM 48) this fine dining establishment has a chic atmosphere and expansive views of the ocean. Fresh fish and sushi are highlighted in their menu, which combines Asian and Caribbean tastes. Savor their inventive rolls, nigiri, and sashimi in addition to other mouth-watering delicacies like lobster thermidor and grilled grouper.

**Sweet Treats and Local Specialties:**

Sweet Savannah's Bake Shop: (MM 53.5) Sweet treats and regional specialties Key Lime Pie, cakes, cookies, and pastries are just a few of the freshly made treats available in this little bakery to satisfy your sweet taste.

Coffee Shop Marathon: (MM 53) Enjoy a hearty breakfast and a cup of freshly roasted coffee at this Marathon mainstay to start your day. Throughout the day, they also provide salads, sandwiches, and other light fare.

Marathon offers a wide range of gastronomic options to suit every preference and price range. You will undoubtedly find the ideal eating experience on this island paradise, regardless of your preferences for foreign cuisine, fresh seafood, or a laid-back bite to eat while taking in the scenery.

# Accommodations

Marathon has a wide variety of lodging options that fit the requirements and budget of any family. This island paradise offers the ideal home away from home, whether you're looking for a large resort with kid-friendly facilities, a roomy vacation rental with a private pool, or an affordable hotel with quick access to the beach.

**Resorts that are family-friendly:**

(MM 61). Hawks Cay Resort With a range of lodging options, including roomy villas and apartments with several bedrooms, this large resort provides a genuine family holiday experience. Savor a range of water activities, a kids' club, a saltwater lagoon, and many pools. Additionally, Hawks Cay has a marina, a spa, and eating options on the premises.

(MM 48.5) Tranquility Bay Beach House Resort Spacious beach homes with individual balconies and fully equipped kitchens are available at this resort on the beach, which provides a laid-back vibe. Take advantage of a waterslide, several pools, a private beach, and a range of age-appropriate activities. Additionally, Tranquility Bay has a spa and restaurant on the premises.

**Vacation Rental for Family Fun:**

Family-Friendly Vacation Homes: Roomy Houses with Private Pools: Look for vacation homes that are ideal for gatherings of friends or family, with private pools, complete kitchens, and several bedrooms. Savor the seclusion and adaptability of owning your own area, which often includes features like gaming rooms, outside barbecues, and laundry rooms. (Prices vary.)

Oceanfront Condos: Pick a condominium with breath-taking views of the ocean and resort-style facilities including fitness centres, hot tubs, and pools. Condos are a handy and cozy choice for families looking for a homey atmosphere. (Prices vary.)

**Low-Cost Accommodations:**

Marathon Motel & RV Park: (MM 52.5) this family-friendly hotel is conveniently located close to Sombrero Beach and provides cozy and reasonably priced lodging along with a playground and pool. For those who are traveling with their own recreational vehicle, their RV park also provides complete hook-ups.

Resort at Coconut Cay: (MM 49.5) this inexpensive resort has a private beach, a pool, and a range of water activities in a laid-back setting. Select from cozy guest rooms, apartments with kitchenettes, or efficiency.

**Beyond the Basics:**

Curry Hammock State Park Camping (MM 56.2) Consider camping in Curry Hammock State Park for a special family outing. Savor a beachside setting while kayaking through mangroves and taking in the Florida Keys' breath-taking natural surroundings.

Marathon has a range of accommodation choices to guarantee a relaxing and unforgettable stay on this island paradise, regardless of your family's requirements or financial constraints.

# Nightlife

Marathon's laid-back vibe is perfect for unwinding after a day in the Keys, despite its lack of nightlife. Whether you're looking for a laid-back waterfront bar, a pleasant pub environment, or live music, Marathon has plenty of places to spend the evening.

**Pubs and local bars:**

The landing of Sparky: (MM 47.5) A local favorite, this waterfront pub and restaurant offers a laid-back vibe along with breath-taking sunset views. Savor a cuisine that includes American staples and fresh seafood, a large assortment of beers on tap, and live music on some evenings.

Keys Marina & Fisheries Market: (MM 49) Keys Fisheries is more than simply a fish store; it also has a fun bar with a laid-back vibe. Savor a refreshing beverage while seeing the passing fishing vessels or stop by for a snack from their informal menu.

MM 49: The Hurricane This iconic Keys pub has a nautical motif and a relaxed vibe. Savor a large assortment of beers, beverages, and a cuisine that includes regional specialties and pub food.

## Venues for Live Music:

Lazy Days South: (MM 50.5) on certain evenings, local artists performing a range of genres perform live at this pub and restaurant on the lake. Savor a tropical beverage on their large terrace with a view of the ocean while taking in live music.

Porky's Bayside Barbecue & Smokehouse (MM 47.5) on certain nights, this laid-back restaurant with views of the harbor also has live music. In a laid-back atmosphere, savor their mouth-watering BBQ and regional artisan brews while taking in live music.

## Additional Nightlife Choices:

- The Marathon Community Theatre's Movie Night (MM 51) Visit this outdoor cinema to see a film beneath the stars. They have a range of movies all week long, which makes it an enjoyable and reasonably priced choice for a night out.
- Stargazing: Marathon provides great chances for stargazing because of the low levels of light pollution. See the stars in a park or on a remote beach.

The key to Marathon's nightlife scene is to embrace the laid-back atmosphere of the island. You'll find the ideal location to have a wonderful evening in this little island town, whether you're searching for live music, a welcoming ambiance, or just a place to relax with a refreshing drink.

# Water Activities

Marathon is a popular destination for water sports because of its central Florida Keys location. There is an aquatic activity for every interest and ability level, including world-class fishing, colorful coral reefs, and serene kayaking courses.

**Charters for fishing:**

Fishing in the Deep Sea: Deep-sea fishing in Marathon is well-known, offering the chance to capture valuable game species like mahi mahi, sailfish, tuna, and marlin. To pursue your prize catch, charter a boat with a skilled captain and crew to traverse the Gulf Stream and offshore reefs.

**Insider Tip:** Fly fishing, light tackle, and deep-sea fishing are among the half-day or full-day excursions that several charters provide. Especially during the busiest times of the year, try making reservations in advance.

Wilderness fishing: For a unique fishing experience, go into the shallow waters of Florida Bay and the wilderness of Everglades

National Park. In these pristine habitats, target species such as redfish, permit, tarpon, and bonefish.

**Insider Tip:** To negotiate the shallow waters and get knowledgeable guidance on methods and local laws, hire a guide with experience in wilderness fishing.

**Trips for snorkeling and diving:**

Sombrero Reef: snorkelers and divers should not miss this famous reef, which is identified by a historic lighthouse. Discover vivid coral formations, swim with colorful fish, and come across amazing animals like moray eels and marine turtles.

**Insider Tip:** For a safer and more educational experience, choose a guided diving or snorkeling excursion. Numerous operators provide equipment and knowledgeable advice for visits to Sombrero Reef.

**Additional Dive Websites:** Many more diving locations, including the Delta Shoal, Coffins Patch, and the Thunderbolt shipwreck (an artificial reef), are accessible from Marathon.

**Insider Tip:** Based on your interests and degree of expertise, ask local dive shops for suggestions. Additionally, they may provide details on required equipment and certifications.

**Kayaking:**

Calm Investigation: Paddle along the calm waters of the Gulf of Mexico or Florida Bay, which are fringed by mangroves. See a variety of birds, get up close and personal with marine life such as dolphins and manatees, and take in the tranquility of nature.

*Insider Tip: For a more educational experience, think about taking a guided kayak trip or renting kayaks from nearby outfitters.*

Curry Hammock State Park: This park provides access to remote beaches and well-marked kayaking paths through mangrove woods.

*Insider Tip: Bring your own kayak or check the park's concession booth for kayak rentals.*

Discovering Sombrero Reef: Snorkeling and Diving: With its modest depths and colorful coral formations brimming with marine life, Sombrero Reef is a top snorkeling and diving destination.

*Insider Tip: For a hassle-free experience with equipment supplied and knowledgeable supervision, sign up for a guided tour.*

Boat trips: A number of companies provide boat trips to Sombrero Reef, which let you take in the natural splendor and see marine life while lounging in a boat.

*Insider Tip: For a more engaging experience, choose a trip that offers possibilities for diving or snorkeling.*

Exploration of the Lighthouse: Although the actual lighthouse is closed to the public, you may see its historic architecture and discover its importance from a distance.

*Insider Tip: Use a boat or kayak to take breath-taking pictures of the lighthouse and the surrounding reef.*

Marathon provides many chances for exploration and adventure with its variety of water sports. This island paradise offers the ideal aquatic experience, whether you're looking for excitement or peace.

# Chapter 6: Big Pine Key & the Lower Keys

## Top Attractions

Travel to the Lower Keys, where unspoiled natural beauty and a slower pace of life are paramount. For environment lovers, animal enthusiasts, and those looking for a peaceful getaway from the everyday, Big Pine Key and the nearby islands provide a sanctuary.

**Key Deer Refuge National:**

A Sanctuary for Miniature Deer: The Key deer, the smallest subspecies of North American white-tailed deer, is protected on this 9,200-acre preserve. These friendly animals, who are a little larger than a large dog, are allowed to graze freely on the islands that encircle the preserve.

- Visitor Centre: Learn about the refuge's goals, its distinctive ecology, and the Key deer conservation initiatives by stopping by the visitor centre.
- Wildlife Viewing: For the greatest chance of seeing Key deer and other wildlife like birds, butterflies, and reptiles, drive slowly along the refuge roads or stroll the nature paths.

**Realistic Specifics:**

- Hours: Open every day from sunrise to sunset.
- Admission is free.
- Accessibility: Wheelchair users may reach the visitor centre and some trails.

## Honda State Park in Bahia

Beach Bliss: With immaculate white sand, glistening blue seas, and swaying palm trees, this park is home to some of the most stunning beaches in the Florida Keys. Build sandcastles with the family, swim in the serene seas, or just unwind on the beach.

- Discover the gorgeous coral reefs right offshore, alive with a variety of fish and marine life, at snorkeling Paradise. Bring your own snorkeling equipment or rent it from the park's concession kiosk.
- Historic Bridge: Enjoy breath-taking views of the surrounding waterways while strolling or cycling over the Old Bahia Honda Bridge, a historic monument.

**Realistic Specifics:**

- Hours: Everyday from 8:00 AM till dusk.
- Fees: $8 per car.
- Accessibility: Restrooms and beaches are wheelchair-accessible.

**The Hole in Blue:**

Unique Ecosystem: Originally a rock hole, this freshwater quarry has developed into a unique ecosystem that is home to a wide range of creatures. See birds, turtles, alligators, and other animals that live in this oasis.

- Platform for Observation: A viewing platform offers a secure and convenient location from which to observe the fauna.
- Nature route: There are chances for birding and nature photography along this brief nature route that runs through the nearby hardwood hammock.

**Realistic Specifics:**

- Hours: Morning to evening.
- Admission is free.
- Accessibility: Wheelchair users may partly reach the route and viewing deck.

**Beyond the Highlights:**

No Name Key: Take a detour to this remote island, renowned for its relaxed vibe and distinctive fauna. Enjoy the peace and quiet of this undiscovered treasure, see Key deer, and stop by the No Name Pub.

Discover Looe Key National Marine Sanctuary, a beautiful coral reef known for its abundant marine life and top-notch diving and snorkeling conditions. Experience this underwater beauty by renting a boat or going on a guided trip.

The Lower Keys provide a special fusion of peaceful getaways, animal encounters, and scenic splendor. Discover the pristine appeal of this island paradise by exploring these alluring attractions.

## Dining & Cuisine:

Like the islands themselves, the Lower Keys provide a casual and simple gastronomic experience. Local products, fresh seafood, and a dash of "Keys Cuisine" combine to offer a distinctive eating experience that captures the laid-back vibe and closeness to the sea of the area.

### Views of the Waterfront and New Catch:

MM 25: Summerland Key is home to Monte's Restaurant & Marina, a legendary eatery that has been there since 1948 and is a real Lower Keys institution. Enjoy fresh off-the-boat seafood, such as their well-known cracked conch, lobster, and stone crab claws (when available), while dining on their waterfront deck. Make sure to try their Key Lime Pie, which is cooked using a family recipe that has been handed down through the years.

Looe Key Reef Resort & Dive Centre Restaurant: (MM 27.5, Ramrod Key) this laid-back beachfront eatery serves fresh seafood, traditional American fare, and tropical drinks, and it has breath-taking views of the Atlantic Ocean. As the sun sets over the sea, savor their well-known Fish Tacos, Conch Chowder, and Key Lime Pie.

**Local flavors and casual dining options:**

Big Pine Restaurant (MM 30, Big Pine Key) is a laid-back, family-friendly eatery with a varied cuisine that includes local delicacies, American classics, and fresh seafood. Savor their well-liked Key Lime Pie, Conch Fritters, and Fish & Chips.

No Name Tavern: (No Name Key) Take a detour to this iconic tavern, which is only reachable by boat or a lengthy, picturesque drive. Savor their well-known pizza, burgers, and regional craft beers in a laid-back setting.

**Keys Cuisine with a Twist:**

Boondocks Grille & Draft House: (MM 27.5, Ramrod Key) this laid-back eatery specializes in "Floribbean," which combines Floridian and Caribbean ingredients. Savor their inventive offerings, such as Key Lime Pie with a Graham cracker crust, Conch Fritters with mango salsa, and Jerk Chicken.

Mangrove Mama's: (MM 20, Sugarloaf Key) this relaxed eatery provides a distinctive dining experience emphasizing locally produced products and sustainably farmed fish. Key Lime Pie with a macadamia nut crust, Coconut Curry Shrimp, and Grilled Mahi-Mahi with mango salsa are some of the delicacies on their menu.

**Island Delights & Sweet Treats:**

Sugarloaf resort: MM 17, Sugarloaf Key. This little resort has a laid back restaurant with a cuisine that includes American classics, fresh fish, and delectable desserts. Savor their well-known Key Lime Pie, which has a tart filling and a handmade Graham cracker crust.

Baby's Coffee: (MM 30, Big Pine Key) This Big Pine Key staple is a wonderful place to start the day with a cup of locally roasted coffee and a hearty breakfast. Throughout the day, they also provide salads, sandwiches, and other light fare.

The gastronomic experience in the Lower Keys is as varied as the islands themselves. You may discover the ideal eating experience to sate your appetites, whether it's casual dining, fresh seafood with views of the coastline, or Keys cuisine with a twist.

# Accommodations

Choose lodgings that put sustainability and environmental harmony first to embrace the Lower Keys' eco-conscious culture.

There are several alternatives available that let you take in the beauty of this island paradise while reducing your effect, from eco-friendly resorts to rustic camping.

**Sustainable Resorts:**

Little Palm Island Resort & Spa: (Little Torch Key) This opulent private island resort is dedicated to eco-friendly techniques, such as using locally produced products, conserving water, and using solar energy. Enjoy the comfort of barefoot living while reducing your environmental impact. Savor exquisite restaurants, a world-class spa, a spotless beach, and private bungalows.

The family-friendly Looe Key Reef Resort & Dive Centre (Ramrod Key) has a laid-back vibe and emphasizes ecotourism. Water conservation, recycling initiatives, and the usage of biodegradable cleaning supplies are among their top priorities. Savor a range of water activities, a diving facility, a pool, and a private beach.

**Green-themed vacation rentals:**

Off-Grid Eco-Cottages: Look for vacation homes with composting, solar, and rainwater collecting systems. These environmentally friendly lodgings provide a special chance to live sustainably while still having all the conveniences of home. (Prices vary.)

Sustainable Features of Oceanfront Homes: Pick a vacation rental with features like water conservation systems, solar panels, and energy-efficient appliances. Take in breath-taking views of the ocean while reducing your environmental footprint. (Prices vary.)

**Nature Lovers' Campsites:**

Camp under the stars in Bahia Honda State Park, a stunning state park renowned for its immaculate beaches and colorful coral reefs. Either basic tent sites or campsites with power and water connections are available. Take pleasure in kayaking, swimming, snorkeling, and discovering the park's natural splendor.

With access to a marina, a pool, and a range of water activities, Sunshine Key RV Resort & Marina (Ohio Key) provides a unique chance to camp on a private island. Water conservation and recycling initiatives are among their top priorities.

**Beyond the Basics:**

- Volunteer Opportunities: To help preserve the local ecology, think about working with groups like the Florida Keys National Marine Sanctuary or the Reef Environmental Education Foundation (REEF).
- Support Local Businesses: Pick environmentally conscious tour companies, eateries, and retail establishments that value sustainable operations and give back to the neighborhood.

Selecting environmentally friendly lodging and encouraging sustainable travel can help protect the Lower Keys' natural splendor for future generations.

# Nightlife

The Lower Keys' nightlife scene mirrors the same relaxed vibe, making it a welcome respite from the bustling. Cozy pubs, welcoming bars, and an emphasis on savoring enjoyable company and the little joys of island life will replace bustling clubs and packed dance floors.

**Pubs and local bars:**

No Name Pub: (No Name Key) this iconic venue is a must-see because of its unique vibe and small-town charm. It is more than simply a bar; it is a place where people congregate and has a past as vibrant as its walls, which are covered with souvenirs and dollar notes. Savor their renowned pizza and regional artisan brews, play pool, and take in live music on the weekends.

Big Pine Key Fishing Lodge: (MM 33, Big Pine Key) after a day of fishing or island exploration, relax at this laid-back lodge with a welcoming bar. Enjoy a refreshing drink in a laid-back atmosphere while chatting with locals and exchanging experiences. Their outside terrace is a wonderful place to take in the island air and watch the sunset.

The Square Grouper Bar & Grill: (MM 22.5, Cudjoe Key) This well-known eatery and bar has a vibrant environment and sometimes has live music. With its breath-taking views, their waterfront balcony is a perfect spot to sip cocktails and take in the island atmosphere. A late-night menu with delectable bar snacks and regional specialties is also available.

Boondocks Grille & Draft House: (MM 27.5, Ramrod Key) This laid-back eatery and bar specializes in "Floribbean" food and locally brewed craft beers in a laid-back atmosphere. Savor their outdoor terrace, weekend live music, and welcoming environment for both residents and tourists.

**Local hangouts and hidden gems:**

The hidden gem Cudjoe Gardens Marina & Restaurant (MM 21, Cudjoe Key) is a beachfront bar with a relaxed vibe and breathtaking sunset views. Savor a refreshing beverage while observing the passing boats, or stop by for a bite to eat from their menu, which offers both local favorites and fresh seafood.

The Looe Key Reef Resort's laid-back tiki bar, The Looe Key Tiki Bar (MM 27.5, Ramrod Key), has tropical beverages and live music on some evenings. It's a perfect spot to relax after diving or snorkeling all day.

**Beyond the Bars:**

Beach bonfires: The Lower Keys' many beaches permit bonfires providing a special chance to get together with loved ones, toast marshmallows, and take in the night sky. Before lighting a bonfire, make sure you are in compliance with local laws and secure all required licenses.

Stargazing: The Lower Keys provide excellent chances for stargazing because of the low levels of light pollution. See the stars in a park or on a remote beach.

Embracing the laid-back pace of island living is key to the Lower Keys' night-time culture. You'll find the ideal location to have a wonderful evening in this peaceful paradise, whether you're looking for live music, a welcoming ambiance, or just a place to relax with a refreshing drink.

# Water Activities

For those looking for aquatic experiences, the Lower Keys provide a beautiful and varied marine environment. Every water lover may have an amazing time exploring isolated islands and colorful coral reefs or canoeing through serene mangrove woods.

**Exploring Mangrove Forests via Kayaking:**

Discover Hidden Waterways: Take a kayaking excursion through the Lower Keys' complex system of mangrove canals and tunnels. These distinct habitats provide a tranquil haven from the open ocean and refuge to a wide range of marine creatures.

*Insider Tip: For a more educational experience, rent kayaks from nearby outfitters or sign up for a guided tour. Guides may share their expertise in ecology, identify species, and point out secret coves.*

Popular Locations: There are excellent kayaking options at Bahia Honda State Park, National Key Deer Refuge, and the seas around No Name Key.

*Insider Tip: Observe the variety of birds, such as ospreys, egrets, and herons, while paddling silently. In the shallows, you may even see a Key deer or a manatee wading.*

**Fishing**

Wilderness fishing: There are great fishing chances in the wilderness of Everglades National Park and the shallow waters of Florida Bay. In these pristine habitats, target species such as redfish, permit, tarpon, and bonefish.

*Insider Tip: To negotiate the shallow waters and get knowledgeable guidance on methods and local laws, hire a guide with experience in wilderness fishing.*

Cast a line from any of the Lower Keys' many bridges, such as the famous Seven Mile Bridge, to engage in bridge fishing. Take in the breath-taking scenery while attempting to capture reef fish, such as groupers and snapper.

*Insider Tip: Verify the fishing laws in your area and, if necessary, get a license.*

**Snorkeling:**

Discover the beautiful coral reef known for its abundant marine life and excellent snorkeling conditions at Looe Key National Marine Sanctuary. Discover a variety of coral formations, sea turtles, and vibrant fish in this underwater paradise.

*Insider Tip: For a hassle-free experience with equipment supplied and knowledgeable direction, sign up for a guided snorkeling trip.*

Bahia Honda State Park: Explore a range of marine life, such as colorful fish, sea turtles, and even the odd stingray, while snorkeling the placid waters off the park's beaches.

*Insider Tip: Bring your own snorkeling equipment or rent it from the park's concession shop.*

**Exploring Remote Islands:**

No Name Key: Take a detour to this remote island, which is only reachable by boat or a lengthy, picturesque drive. Visit the renowned No Name Pub, take in the peace and quiet of its beaches, and discover the distinctive ecology.

*Insider Tip: To explore No Name Key's remote covers and mangrove-lined canals, rent a kayak or paddleboard.*

Visit the pristine island of Lignumvitae Key Botanical State Park by boat. It is home to a virgin tropical hardwood hammock and a variety of fauna. Explore the island's history, walk through the nature paths, and take in the serene surroundings.

*Insider Tip: Robbie's Marina in Islamorada offers boat cruises to Lignumvitae Key.*

Discover the remains of Indian Key Historic State Park, a once-thriving island that was used as a wrecker's town in the 1800s. Discover the history of the island, take in the natural beauty of this historic location, and snorkel the nearby seas.

*Insider Tip: Robbie's Marina in Islamorada offers boat cruises to Indian Key.*

The Lower Keys provide many chances for aquatic adventures because of their beautiful seas, varied ecosystems, and isolated islands. This island paradise offers the ideal water activity to make lifelong memories, whether you're looking for excitement or peace.

# Chapter 7: Key West

## Top Attractions

The southernmost city in the continental United States, Key West, has a fascinating mix of rich culture, historical importance, and relaxed island charm. Here is a sneak peek at a few of its well-known attractions, each of which provides discriminating tourists with a distinctive experience:

**Mallory Square:** Malcolm Square becomes a hive of activity as the sun sets, creating a breath-taking sunset spectacle. The Sunset Celebration is a weekly event that attracts both residents and tourists to see an amazing show of singers, artists, and street performers. While local merchants sell delicious foods and homemade goods, jugglers, tightrope walkers, and singers create a joyful atmosphere.

Arrival Strategy: Get there at least an hour early to guarantee a favorable place to see the sunset. This gives you plenty of time to browse the nearby stores and take in the lively ambiance.

**Waterfront Promenade:** Mallory Square doubles as a charming waterfront promenade outside of the sunset festivities. Admire the historic architecture that symbolizes Key West's rich history as you stroll down the pier, which is dotted with quaint stores and eateries.

**Useful Points to Remember:**

- Every day, the Sunset Celebration begins around two hours before the sun sets.
- Accessibility: All tourists may use the square since it is wheelchair accessible.

**Duval Street:**

The Island's Lively Artery: Duval Street, the beating centre of Key West, is a busy street dotted with a diverse array of stores, eateries, pubs, and historical sites. A snapshot of the island's dynamic energy and diversified culture may be found on this busy street.

Enjoy some shopping therapy at the many stores that line Duval Street. Find distinctive mementos, regional artwork, upscale stores, and well-known brands. A tribute to the island's marine past, the Key West Sponge Market offers a wide selection of natural sponges and bath goods. Don't miss it.

Gastronomic delights: With a variety of eating options, Duval Street's gastronomic scene is as varied as its stores. There is something for every taste, ranging from sophisticated seafood grills and foreign cuisine to laid-back cafés and real Cuban eateries.

Nightlife Enclave: Duval Street becomes a bustling centre of nightlife as the sun sets. Discover a range of pubs, taverns, and live music venues, each with a distinct atmosphere and selection of entertainment.

**Useful Points to Remember:**

- Accessibility: Most of Duval Street's stores and eateries are wheelchair accessible.

**Home & Museum of Ernest Hemingway:**

A Literary Sanctuary: Enter the old Key West home of one of America's most renowned writers, Ernest Hemingway. With guided tours that shed light on his writing process and the sources of inspiration he found on the island, this exquisitely kept home offers a window into his life and career.

A colony of polydactyl (six-toed) cats, descended from Hemingway's personal beloved cat, Snow White, also resides on the site. These endearing cats contribute to the museum's own personality.

**Useful Points to Remember:**

- Operation hours are 9:00 AM to 5:00 PM every day.
- Adult admission is $17.
- Accessibility: The house's historical significance limits its accessibility.

## Historic Fort Zachary Taylor State Park:

A Look Back: Discover the military history of Key West at this Civil War-era fort, which is a National Historic Landmark. The building of the fort, its involvement in the Civil War, and its strategic importance are all covered in guided tours.

Coastal Oasis: In addition to its historical value, Fort Zachary Taylor is home to a spotless beach with glistening waves and fantastic snorkeling spots. Explore the underwater world filled with marine life, swim in the cool seas, or just unwind on the beach.

## Useful Points to Remember:

- Operation hours are 8:00 AM to sundown every day.
- Admission: $6 per car.
- Accessibility: Restrooms and beaches are wheelchair-accessible.

A fascinating fusion of culture, history, and scenic beauty can be found in Key West. Discover these well-known sites and lose yourself in this island paradise's distinct charm.

# Dining & Cuisine

The eating options in Key West are as varied and lively as the island itself, ranging from sophisticated waterfront eateries to laid-back Cuban cafés and everything in between. There is something for every palette in Key West's varied culinary scene, whether you're in the mood for a romantic supper, a quick lunch, or a taste of the local cuisine.

**Local Flavors & Casual Bites:**

For more than 50 years, the family-run El Siboney Restaurant (900 Catherine St.) has been a mainstay in Key West, offering traditional Cuban fare including picadillo and Cuban sandwiches. Savor their tasty meals at reasonable costs in a relaxed setting.

B.O.'s Fish Wagon: (801 Caroline St) This well-known Key West restaurant specializes in fresh seafood and has a laid-back, eccentric vibe. Savor local specialties like conch fritters and their renowned fish sandwiches.

Stands for Conch Fritters: A visit to Key West wouldn't be complete without sampling some conch fritters. You can get these golden, crispy fritters from food trucks and booths all around the island. Try a few stands to discover your favorite, since each has its own special recipe.

**Waterfront dining with a View:**

Latitudes: (Sunset Key) Only reachable by boat, this fine dining establishment provides a really exceptional dining experience with stunning views of the Gulf of Mexico. Savor their elegant cuisine, which includes excellent steaks, fresh seafood, and tropical drinks.

The Ocean Key Resort & Spa's Hot Tin Roof is a rooftop restaurant that provides breath-taking views of the Key West bay and sunset. Savor meals like lobster risotto and grilled mahi-mahi in their modern American cuisine with Caribbean flavors.

### Fine Dining and International Cuisine:

The highly regarded Italian eatery Antonia's (615 Duval St.) provides a classy dining experience emphasizing seasonal, fresh ingredients. Savor their large wine selection, wood-fired pizzas, and homemade pasta.

Seven Fish (632 Olivia St) this little eatery serves inventive dishes made with regional ingredients and fresh fish. Savor their creatively prepared food in a romantic setting.

Azur: (425 Grinnell St.) This classy restaurant specializes in local vegetables and fresh seafood, serving Mediterranean-inspired cuisine. Savor their exquisite atmosphere and breath-taking courtyard location.

### Key Lime Pie & Sweet Treats:

A staple of Key West, Kermit's Key West Key Lime Shoppe has many locations and serves a range of Key lime pie varieties, including conventional, chocolate-dipped, and even Key lime pie on a stick. Don't forget to try their other lime-inspired sweets, which include ice cream, pastries, and candy.

Blue Heaven: 729 Thomas St. This well-known restaurant and bar has a verdant garden and a laid-back vibe. Savor their delectable Key lime pie, which has a tart filling and a handmade Graham cracker crust.

From light nibbles to elegant dining experiences, Key West's varied culinary culture has something to offer everyone. Discover the tastes that make Key West a veritable culinary paradise by visiting the island's eateries.

## Accommodations

A wide range of lodging options are available in Key West, which reflects the island's unique character. After a day of seeing this fascinating island, you'll discover the ideal spot to relax, whether you're looking for opulent treatment, historical charm, or a comfortable haven.

**Luxury resorts:**

Constructed in the 1920s, Casa Marina Key West, Curio Collection by Hilton (1500 Reynolds St) is a magnificent and elegant landmark. Savor a private beach, several pools, an opulent spa, and breath-taking views of the ocean. Private cottages, apartments, or roomy guest rooms are available.

Situated on Duval Street, The Reach Key West, Curio Collection by Hilton: (1435 Simonton St.) This chic resort provides convenient access to the island's attractions and lively nightlife. Savor a range of culinary choices, a rooftop pool, and a private beach.

With a wonderful position at the end of Duval Street, Ocean Key Resort & Spa offers breath-taking waterfront views and convenient access to the island's attractions. Savor a range of eating choices, a private beach, several pools, and a top-notch spa.

## Historic Guesthouses:

The Gardens Hotel (526 Angela St) this little guesthouse provides a peaceful haven from the bustle of Duval Street, tucked away in a beautiful tropical garden. Take advantage of their free breakfast, cool pool, and ancient architecture.

Marquesa Hotel: Situated in a tastefully renovated Victorian mansion, (600 Fleming St.) is a sophisticated lodging option that combines contemporary amenities with a touch of history. Take advantage of their free breakfast, cool pool, and verdant courtyard.

## Boutique Hotels:

With a marina, a pool, and a range of water activities, the Perry Hotel Key West (7001 Shrimp Rd) is a chic boutique hotel on Stock Island that provides a distinctive waterfront experience. Savor their contemporary decor, laid-back vibe, and breath-taking sunset vistas.

Ocean's Edge Key West Hotel & Marina (5950 Peninsular Ave) This modern hotel has a private beach, a marina, and a range of water activities in a laid-back setting. Savor their roomy guest rooms, cool pool, and breath-taking views of the seaside.

### Rentals for Vacations:

- Conch Cottages: Savor the allure of Key West in a classic conch cottage, which provides a comfortable and genuine island setting. (Prices vary.)
- Luxurious Villas: Savor roomy villas with gourmet kitchens, private pools, and breath-taking views of the ocean. (Prices vary.)
- Historic Homes: Take a unique look into Key West's history by staying in a tastefully restored historic house. (Prices vary.)

Every taste and price range is catered to by Key West's many accommodation alternatives. You may locate the ideal lodging to make the most of your Key West trip, whether you're looking for opulent indulgence, historic charm, or a comfortable haven.

# Nightlife

After dusk, Key West is a flurry of activity, laughter, and music. This island city takes pride in its reputation for having a thriving nightlife, providing a culture that is inclusive and varied enough to suit all tastes. Key West offers something for everyone, whether you're looking for drag performances, live music, dancing, or just a fun ambiance to experience the island sensations.

**Live Music Hotspots:**

Sloppy Joe's Bar: (201 Duval St) This iconic bar is a Key West institution and was formerly visited by Ernest Hemingway. Every night, take in a mix of rock, reggae, and island music performed by local bands. Sloppy Joe's is a must-visit for every nightlife aficionado because of its vibrant atmosphere and historical importance.

Green Parrot Bar: (601 Whitehead St) This well-liked neighborhood bar is renowned for its diverse live music selection, which includes jazz, funk, reggae, and blues. With its laid-back vibe and eclectic clientele, The Green Parrot is a wonderful place to get a refreshing drink and take in the island beats.

Every day, local and traveling musicians of many genres perform live at the well-known pub and restaurant Hog's Breath Saloon (400 Front St). Savor their large outdoor terrace, views of the waterfront, and a vibrant ambiance that keeps the party going into the wee hours of the morning.

**Drag Shows and Nightlife for LGBTQ+ People:**

The famous gay club 801 Bourbon Club, located at 801 Duval St., is a mainstay of Key West and features weekly drag performances with amazing performers and a vibrant environment. Savor their large dance floor, many bars, and inclusive atmosphere.

711 Duval St. is home to the well-known LGBTQ+ nightclub Aqua, which features drag performances, dancing, and DJs in an exciting environment. Their varied music choices and numerous levels appeal to a wide range of preferences.

La Te Da: (1125 Duval St) this classy restaurant and bar has live music and cabaret performances in a sophisticated setting. Their drag performances are renowned for their skillful actors and lavish costumes.

**Pubs & bars with a distinct feel:**

A Key West icon, Captain Tony's Saloon (428 Greene St.) was once a cigar factory and a morgue. Savor their distinctive ambiance, live music, and extensive beer and beverage menu.

The Schooner Wharf Tavern, located at 202 William St., is a laid-back waterfront tavern with live music, a welcoming clientele, and breath-taking sunset views. Enjoy a refreshing drink and take in the tropical atmosphere at this spot.

Garden of Eden: (224 Duval St.) This rooftop garden and bar provides a distinctive and freeing experience, and no clothes are required. Savor their vibrant ambiance, expansive vistas, and an opportunity to unwind and enjoy the essence of the Key West.

The nightlife of Key West is a colorful tapestry of entertainment, music, and individuality. In this fascinating city, you're sure to find the ideal location whether you're looking for a fun party, a cultural adventure, or just somewhere to relax and take in the island atmosphere.

# Water Activities

Key West's crystal-clear turquoise waters and diverse marine ecosystems beckon adventurers to explore its underwater wonders and enjoy thrilling activities on the surface. From vibrant coral reefs to exhilarating jet ski rides, there's an aquatic experience for every taste and skill level.

**Snorkeling and Diving:**

Coral Reef Exploration: Immerse yourself in the underwater world of the Florida Keys National Marine Sanctuary, a haven for diverse marine life. Snorkel or dive at renowned reefs like the Eastern Dry Rocks, Sand Key, and Western Sambo, encountering colorful fish, sea turtles, and fascinating coral formations.

*Insider Tip: Join a guided snorkeling or diving tour for a hassle-free experience with provided equipment and expert guidance.*

Shipwreck Adventures: For experienced divers, Key West offers opportunities to explore historic shipwrecks, like the USS Vandenberg (a former missile-tracking ship) and the Cayman Salvager (a cargo vessel).

*Insider Tip: Ensure you have the necessary certifications and experience for wreck diving.*

**Sunset Cruises:** Romantic Escapes: Sail into the sunset aboard a catamaran or sailboat, enjoying breath-taking views of the Key West skyline and the vibrant colors of the sky. Many cruises offer complimentary drinks and appetizers, creating a perfect romantic setting.

Party Vibes: For a more lively experience, join a sunset cruise with live music, dancing, and a festive atmosphere. These cruises often include an open bar and snacks, making it a fun way to celebrate with friends.

**Kayaking:** Tranquil Exploration: Paddle through the mangrove-lined waterways and explore the backcountry of Key West. Observe diverse birdlife, encounter marine creatures like dolphins and manatees, and enjoy the peaceful serenity of the natural environment.

*Insider Tip: Rent kayaks from local outfitters or join a guided kayak tour for a more informative experience.*

**Jet Skiing:** Thrilling Rides: Experience the exhilaration of jet skiing through the crystal-clear waters of Key West. Many rental companies offer guided tours, allowing you to explore secluded beaches, and mangrove islands, and even encounter dolphins.

*Insider Tip: follow safety guidelines and respect speed limits to ensure a safe and enjoyable experience.*

**Parasailing:** Bird's-Eye Views: Soar above the turquoise waters and enjoy breath-taking panoramic views of Key West and the surrounding islands. Parasailing offers a unique perspective of the island's beauty and a thrilling adventure for adrenaline seekers.

*Insider Tip: Choose a reputable parasailing company with experienced operators and safety measures in place.*

**Other Water Activities:**

- Paddle boarding: Enjoy a leisurely paddle boarding excursion through the calm waters of Key West, offering a relaxing way to explore the coastline and observe marine life.

- Windsurfing and Kitesurfing: Key West offers excellent conditions for windsurfing and kitesurfing. For those seeking a more challenging water sport, you may rent equipment or learn from local professionals.

- Fishing Charters: Embark on a fishing charter and try your luck catching snapper, grouper, and other reef fish. Key West also offers deep-sea fishing expeditions targeting larger game fish.

With its diverse water activities, Key West offers endless opportunities for adventure and exploration. Whether you're seeking thrills or tranquility, you will find the perfect aquatic experience in this island paradise.

# Chapter 8: Museums & Galleries

## Key West Museum of Art & History

Situated within the architectural grandeur of the 1891 Custom House, a National Historic Landmark overlooking Key West Harbor, the Key West Museum of Art & History offers a captivating exploration of the island's vibrant past and artistic legacy.

**Delving into the island's narrative:**

Historical Immersion: The museum's meticulously curated exhibits chronicle Key West's fascinating evolution, from its origins as a humble settlement to its rise as a thriving maritime hub. Visitors are invited to delve into the narratives of shipwrecks and salvaged treasures, the island's pivotal role in the Civil War and World War II, and the cultural tapestry woven by diverse communities, including Cuban immigrants and the vibrant Bahamian Conch community.

Notable Artifacts: Among the museum's treasures are artifacts recovered from shipwrecks, intricate cigar-making tools, 19th-century household items that offer glimpses into daily life, and even personal effects belonging to renowned figures like Ernest Hemingway.

Artistic Expressions: The museum celebrates the island's artistic spirit through a diverse collection that spans various mediums and eras. From the captivating folk art of Mario Sanchez, depicting scenes of everyday life in Key West, to the vibrant textiles of Key West Hand Print fabrics, and the contemporary works of artists inspired by the island's unique landscape and culture, the museum offers a comprehensive perspective on Key West's artistic landscape.

Architectural Significance: The Custom House itself is a testament to Key West's rich architectural heritage. Designed in the Romanesque Revival style, the building boasts intricate details, soaring ceilings, and a grand staircase that transports visitors to a bygone era. The museum's exhibits are thoughtfully integrated within this magnificent structure, enhancing the visitor experience.

**Visitor Information:**

- Address: 281 Front Street, Key West, FL 33040
- Operating Hours: 10:00 AM to 4:00 PM, Tuesday through Saturday (closed Sunday and Monday)
- Admission Fees:
    o Adults: $12
    o Seniors (62+): $10

- ○ Students (with valid ID): $8
- ○ Youth (7-18 years): $6
- ○ Children (6 & under): Free
- Accessibility: The museum is fully wheelchair accessible, with elevators providing access to all exhibition levels.
- Website: www.kwahs.org

**Enhancing Your Museum Experience:**

Guided Tours: For a more in-depth understanding of the museum's collection and Key West's history, guided tours are available. Led by knowledgeable docents, these tours offer valuable insights and enrich the visitor experience.

Special Exhibitions: The museum regularly hosts rotating special exhibitions, featuring diverse themes and artistic expressions. Check the museum's website or inquire at the admissions desk for current and upcoming exhibitions.

Museum Store: The museum store offers a curated selection of unique souvenirs, books, and local art, allowing visitors to take home a piece of Key West's cultural heritage.

The Key West Museum of Art & History is an essential destination for those seeking to delve into the island's captivating past and vibrant artistic spirit. Its thoughtfully curated exhibits, housed within a magnificent architectural gem, provide a rich and rewarding experience for all.

# Mel Fisher Maritime Museum

Step into a world of maritime history and adventure at the Mel Fisher Maritime Museum, a captivating institution that showcases the remarkable discoveries of renowned treasure hunter Mel Fisher and his team. Located in Key West, this museum offers a unique glimpse into the fascinating world of shipwrecks, underwater archaeology, and the stories behind the treasures recovered from the depths.

**A Legacy of Discovery:**

The Atocha Motherlode: The museum's most celebrated exhibit showcases the treasures recovered from the Nuestra Señora de Atocha, a Spanish galleon that sank off the Florida Keys in 1622. Marvel at the dazzling display of gold and silver coins, bars, and ingots, along with precious jewelry, emeralds, and artifacts that offer a glimpse into the opulence of Spain's Golden Age.

Beyond the Atocha: The museum's collection extends beyond the Atocha, featuring artifacts from other significant shipwrecks, including the Santa Margarita (another treasure-laden Spanish galleon), the Henrietta Marie (an English slave ship), and the Santa Clara (a Spanish merchant vessel). These exhibits provide a fascinating glimpse into maritime trade, cultural exchange, and the human stories behind these historical vessels.

**Interactive exhibits and engaging displays:**

Hands-On Exploration: The museum features interactive exhibits that allow visitors to engage with maritime history in a hands-on way. Try your hand at knot tying, explore a replica of a ship's hold, or examine artifacts under a microscope.

Conservation Lab: Witness the meticulous process of conserving and preserving artifacts recovered from shipwrecks. The museum's conservation lab offers a behind-the-scenes look at the intricate work involved in restoring these historical treasures.

Educational Programs: The museum offers a variety of educational programs and events for all ages, including lectures, workshops, and family activities. These programs provide a deeper understanding of maritime history, archaeology, and conservation efforts.

**Visitor Information:**

- Address: 200 Greene Street, Key West, FL 33040
- Operating Hours: 9:30 AM to 5:00 PM daily
- Admission Fees:
    - Adults: $17
    - Seniors (62+): $15
    - Students (with valid ID): $8
    - Youth (6-17 years): $7
    - Children (5 & under): Free

- Accessibility: The museum is fully wheelchair accessible, with elevators providing access to all exhibition levels.

- Website: www.melfisher.org

**Enhancing Your Museum Experience:**

Guided Tours: For a more in-depth understanding of the museum's collection and the stories behind the artifacts, guided tours are available. Led by knowledgeable docents, these tours offer valuable insights and enrich the visitor experience.

Special Exhibitions: The museum regularly hosts rotating special exhibitions, featuring diverse themes related to maritime history, archaeology, and conservation. Check the museum's website or inquire at the admissions desk for current and upcoming exhibitions.

Museum Store: The museum store offers a curated selection of unique souvenirs, books, and replicas of artifacts, allowing visitors to take home a piece of maritime history.

The Mel Fisher Maritime Museum is a must-visit for those seeking to explore the fascinating world of shipwrecks, treasure hunting, and maritime history. Its captivating exhibits, interactive displays, and educational programs provide a rich and rewarding experience for all.

# The Little White House

Step back in time at the Harry S. Truman Little White House, a beautifully preserved presidential retreat that offers a fascinating glimpse into the life and times of one of America's most influential leaders. Located in Key West, this historic home served as President Truman's winter White House for 175 days during his presidency, and it continues to captivate visitors with its rich history and personal stories.

**A Glimpse into Presidential Life:**

Truman's Winter Office: Explore the rooms where President Truman conducted official business, including his private office where he worked on the Marshall Plan and penned the Truman Doctrine. See his original furnishings, personal belongings, and the poker table where he enjoyed games with his staff and dignitaries.

Family Life: Get a sense of the Truman family's life in Key West by exploring their living quarters, including the bedrooms and the sun porch, where they relaxed and entertained guests. See personal items like Bess Truman's sewing machine and the family's collection of books and games.

A Presidential Time Capsule: The Little White House has been meticulously preserved, offering a glimpse into the 1940s and 50s. Admire the original décor, furnishings, and technology of the era, including President Truman's vintage telephone and his 1947 Chrysler Crown Imperial limousine.

**Beyond the Residence:**

Museum Exhibits: The museum features exhibits that delve deeper into President Trump's life and legacy, showcasing his accomplishments, challenges, and personal stories. Learn about his decision to drop the atomic bomb, his role in the Korean War, and his efforts to desegregate the military.

Lush Gardens: Stroll through the lush tropical gardens surrounding the house, enjoying the tranquility and beauty of the natural surroundings. The gardens feature a variety of native plants and flowers, providing a peaceful oasis in the heart of Key West.

**Visitor Information:**

- Address: 111 Front Street, Key West, FL 33040
- Hours of Operation: Daily 9:00 AM to 4:30 PM
- Admission Fees:
    - Adults: $22.45 (includes guided tour)
    - Youth (4-12 years): $10.95 (includes guided tour)
    - Children (3 & under): Free

- Accessibility: The museum is partially wheelchair accessible, with ramps and elevators providing access to most areas. Check with the museum for specific accessibility details.
- Website: www.trumanlittlewhitehouse.org

**Enhancing Your Visit:**

Guided Tours: Guided tours are included with admission and provide valuable insights into President Truman's life, the history of the house, and the significance of the events that took place there.

Special Events: The Little White House hosts various special events throughout the year, including lectures, book signings, and historical re-enactments. A list of forthcoming events may be found on the museum's website.

Museum Store: The museum store offers a curated selection of books, souvenirs, and presidential memorabilia, allowing visitors to take home a piece of history.

The Harry S. Truman Little White House is a must-visit for history buffs, presidential enthusiasts, and anyone interested in experiencing a unique piece of American history. Experience the life and legacy of one of America's most significant leaders by traveling back in time.

## Audubon House & Tropical Gardens

Escape the bustle of Duval Street and step into a tranquil oasis at the Audubon House & Tropical Gardens. This beautifully preserved 19th-century home offers a glimpse into Key West's past and a sanctuary of lush tropical flora.

### Historic Home:

Architectural Gem: Built in the 1840s, the Audubon House is a classic example of Bahamian-style architecture, featuring wide verandas, intricate woodwork, and period furnishings.

Audubon's Legacy: The house is named after renowned naturalist John James Audubon, who visited Key West in 1832 and documented many of the island's bird species. Original Audubon prints are displayed throughout the home.

Geiger Family History: Learn about the Geiger family, who resided in the house for over a century, and their contributions to Key West's maritime history.

### Tropical Gardens:

- Lush Sanctuary: Explore the one-acre tropical garden, a vibrant tapestry of orchids, bromeliads, fruit trees, and other exotic plants.
- Tranquil Escape: Relax by the Koi Pond, wander the brick pathways, and discover hidden nooks within this verdant paradise.
- Historic Kitchen: See the recreated "Cook House," an outdoor kitchen typical of the 1800s.

### Visitor Information:

- Address: 205 Whitehead Street, Key West, FL 33040
- Hours: 9:30 AM to 4:15 PM daily
- Admission: $14 for adults, $6 for children (6-12 years)
- Accessibility: The gardens are wheelchair accessible; the house has limited accessibility.
- Website: audubonhouse.org

### Highlights:

- Guided Tours: Enhance your visit with a guided tour, offering insights into the house's history, architecture, and the Audubon connection.
- Gift Shop: Browse the gift shop for unique souvenirs, books, and Audubon prints.
- Photography: Capture the beauty of the house and gardens with your camera.

The Audubon House & Tropical Gardens offers a captivating blend of history, art, and natural beauty, making it a must-visit for those seeking a tranquil escape in the heart of Key West.

**Marathon**

# Crane Point Museum & Nature Centre

Crane Point Museum & Nature Centre stands as a testament to the ecological and historical richness of the Florida Keys. This 63-acre preserve, located in the heart of Marathon, provides a captivating journey through diverse ecosystems, unique wildlife, and the compelling story of human presence in this island chain.

**Exploring the Natural World:**

Crane Point Hammock: Immerse yourself in the lush tropical hardwood hammock, a rare and vital ecosystem that showcases the biodiversity of the Florida Keys. Towering gumbo limbo trees, majestic mahogany, and intriguing strangler figs create a verdant canopy, providing habitat for a fascinating array of flora and fauna. Observe colorful birds flitting through the foliage, delicate butterflies dancing among the blossoms, and other intriguing creatures that call this hammock home.

Nature Trails: A network of well-maintained nature trails wind through the hammock, inviting exploration and offering opportunities for bird-watching, nature photography, and quiet contemplation amidst the natural splendor.

Tidal Lagoon: Witness the intricate workings of the coastal ecosystem at the tidal lagoon. Observe the fascinating interplay of marine life, including crabs, fish and various invertebrates, as they navigate the fluctuating tides. Gain a deeper understanding of the delicate balance that sustains this unique environment and the importance of conservation efforts.

Marathon Wild Bird Centre: Discover the dedicated work of the Marathon Wild Bird Centre, a rehabilitation facility committed to the rescue and recovery of injured birds. Learn about the challenges faced by these avian creatures and witness the compassionate care provided by the centre's staff. Observe various species up close, including majestic pelicans, graceful herons, and keen-eyed ospreys, as they recuperate and prepare for their return to the wild.

**Unveiling the Past:**

Museum of Natural History: Embark on a journey through time at the Museum of Natural History, where exhibits illuminate the fascinating history of the Florida Keys. Trace the footsteps of the indigenous Calusa people, explore the era of European exploration and settlement, and delve into the stories of pirates, wreckers, and the resilient individuals who shaped the unique cultural tapestry of the Keys.

Adderley House: Step into the past at the historic Adderley House, a meticulously restored 1903 Bahamian-style home. Experience a glimpse into the lifestyle of early Key West settlers as you admire the period furnishings and learn about the family who once inhabited this charming residence.

**Visitor Information:**

- Address: 5550 Overseas Highway, Marathon, FL 33050
- Operating Hours: 9:00 AM to 5:00 PM daily
- Admission Fees:
    o Adults: $15
    o Seniors (62+): $12.50
    o Students (with valid ID): $10
    o Youth (5-13 years): $8
    o Children (4 & under): Free

- Accessibility: The museum, Adderley House, and select trails are wheelchair accessible.
- Website: cranepoint.net

**Enhancing Your Experience:**

- Guided tours: Enhance your understanding of Crane Point's natural and historical significance with a guided tour. Led by knowledgeable naturalists and historians, these tours offer valuable insights and enrich the visitor experience.
- Special Events: Crane Point hosts a variety of special events throughout the year, including nature walks, bird-watching tours, and historical re-enactments. A calendar of forthcoming events may be found on the website.
- Gift Shop: The gift shop offers a curated selection of nature-themed souvenirs, books, and local crafts, allowing visitors to take home a memento of their experience.

Crane Point Museum & Nature Centre is an essential destination for those seeking to explore the natural beauty and rich history of the Florida Keys. Its diverse exhibits, tranquil trails, and educational programs provide a captivating experience for visitors of all ages.

## E.H. Gato Submarine Museum

Step aboard the USS Gato (SS-212) and immerse yourself in the world of World War II submariners at the E.H. Gato Submarine Museum. Located in Marathon, this historic vessel offers a unique opportunity to experience life underwater and gain a deeper appreciation for the brave men who served in the "Silent Service."

**Explore a Wartime submarine:**

Walk the Decks: Explore the Gato's exterior decks, imagining the sights and sounds these sailors would have experienced as they patrolled the Pacific Ocean during World War II. See the conning tower, where the captain commanded the vessel, and the deck gun used for surface attacks.

Descend into the Depths: Venture below deck and enter the cramped quarters of the Gato's interior. See the torpedo tubes, where deadly weapons were launched against enemy ships, and the control room, where the crew navigated and monitored the submarine's systems.

Experience Life Onboard: Explore the crew's mess, where they ate and relaxed, and the bunks where they slept in close quarters. Imagine the challenges and camaraderie of life aboard a submarine during wartime.

Interactive Exhibits: The museum features interactive exhibits that provide further insights into submarine technology, tactics, and the history of the Gato and its crew. Learn about the submarine's Pacific Theater role, dangers, and sacrifices.

**A Historic Vessel:**

World War II Service: The USS Gato was launched in 1941 and served with distinction in the Pacific Theater during World War II. It participated in numerous patrols, sinking enemy ships and rescuing downed pilots.

Post-War Service: After the war, the Gato continued to serve in the U.S. Navy, undergoing modernization and participating in various training exercises. It was decommissioned in 1960 and later transferred to the museum in 1972.

**Visitor Information:**

- Address: 1 Overseas Highway, Marathon, FL 33050 (located at the Pigeon Key Visitor Center)
- Operating Hours: 10:00 AM to 4:00 PM daily (last tour departs at 3:30 PM)
- Admission Fees:
    - Adults: $17
    - Seniors (62+): $15
    - Youth (6-12 years): $9
    - Children (5 & under): Free

- Accessibility: Due to the historic nature of the submarine, access is limited. The main deck and some interior spaces are accessible, but the lower levels and narrow passageways may be challenging for those with mobility issues.
- Website: pigeonkey.net/submarine-museum/

**Enhancing Your Visit:**

Guided Tours: Guided tours are available and highly recommended. Led by knowledgeable volunteers, often former submariners, these tours provide valuable insights into the Gato's history, technology, and the experiences of the crew.

Special Events: The museum hosts special events throughout the year, including re-enactments, veterans' gatherings, and educational programs. A calendar of forthcoming events may be found on the website.

Pigeon Key: The E.H. Gato Submarine Museum is located at the Pigeon Key Visitor Centre, which offers access to the historic island of Pigeon Key. Explore the island's restored buildings, learn about its role in the construction of the Seven Mile Bridge, and enjoy the scenic views.

The E.H. Gato Submarine Museum is a must-visit for history buffs, military enthusiasts, and anyone interested in experiencing life aboard a World War II submarine. Step back in time and gain a deeper appreciation for the brave men who served in the Silent Service.

### Islamorada:

# History of Diving Museum

Dive into the fascinating history of underwater exploration at the History of Diving Museum in Islamorada. This unique museum chronicles humanity's enduring fascination with the underwater world, showcasing the ingenuity and evolution of diving technology from ancient times to the present day.

**A Journey through Time:**

Ancient Beginnings: Discover the earliest forms of diving, from breath-hold diving for pearls and sponges in ancient civilizations to the development of early diving bells and helmets. Explore artifacts like ancient Greek amphorae (used for diving bells) and traditional Japanese Ama diver equipment.

Evolution of Diving Technology: trace the progression of diving technology through the centuries, from Leonardo da Vinci's innovative diving suit designs to the invention of the first practical scuba gear by Jacques Cousteau and Emile Gagnan. See a remarkable collection of antique diving helmets, suits, and breathing apparatus.

Modern Marvels: Explore the advancements in modern diving technology, including re-breathers, mixed gas diving, and underwater robotics. Learn about the pioneers who pushed the boundaries of underwater exploration and the scientific discoveries made possible by these innovations.

**Interactive exhibits and engaging displays:**

Hands-On Experiences: The museum offers interactive exhibits that allow visitors to engage with diving history in a hands-on way. Try on a replica diving helmet, explore a model submarine, or test your knowledge with interactive quizzes.

Rare Artifacts: The museum houses a vast collection of rare and unique artifacts, including antique diving helmets from around the world, vintage underwater cameras, and historical documents related to diving expeditions and discoveries.

Educational Programs: The museum offers a variety of educational programs and events for all ages, including lectures, workshops, and guided tours. These programs provide a deeper understanding of diving history, technology, and the importance of marine conservation.

**Visitor Information:**

- Address: 82990 Overseas Highway, Islamorada, FL 33036
- Operating Hours: 10:00 AM to 5:00 PM daily
- Admission Fees:
    - Adults: $14
    - Seniors (62+): $12
    - Students (with valid ID): $10
    - Youth (6-12 years): $6
    - Children (5 & under): Free

- Accessibility: The museum is wheelchair accessible.
- Website: divingmuseum.org

**Enhancing Your Museum Experience:**

Guided Tours: For a more in-depth understanding of the museum's collection and the history of diving, guided tours are available. Led by knowledgeable docents, these tours offer valuable insights and enrich the visitor experience.

Special Exhibitions: The museum regularly hosts rotating special exhibitions, featuring specific aspects of diving history, technology, or underwater exploration. Check the museum's website or inquire at the admissions desk for current and upcoming exhibitions.

Museum Store: The museum store offers a curated selection of unique souvenirs, books, and diving-related gifts, allowing visitors to take home a piece of underwater history. The History of Diving Museum is a must-visit for diving enthusiasts, history buffs, and anyone curious about the underwater world. Its captivating exhibits, interactive displays, and educational programs provide a fascinating journey through the evolution of underwater exploration.

## Florida Keys History & Discovery Centre

Embark on a captivating journey through time at the Florida Keys History & Discovery Centre a museum dedicated to preserving and showcasing the rich tapestry of events, people, and environments that have shaped this unique island chain. Located in Islamorada, this engaging institution offers a fascinating glimpse into the Keys' diverse history, from its earliest inhabitants to the pioneers who shaped its development.

**Uncovering the Layers of History:**

First Peoples: Discover the legacy of the indigenous Calusa people, who inhabited the Florida Keys for thousands of years before European contact. Learn about their unique culture, their adaptation to the island environment, and their remarkable skills in fishing, canoeing, and building shell mounds.

Pirates and Wreckers: Delve into the intriguing world of pirates and wreckers, who played a significant role in the Keys' early history. Explore the stories of notorious pirates like Black Caesar and Henry Morgan, and learn how the practice of "wrecking"—salvaging goods from shipwrecks—shaped the island's economy and culture.

Spanish Treasure Fleets: Uncover the dramatic history of the Spanish treasure fleets, which sailed through the treacherous Florida Straits laden with gold, silver, and other riches from the New World. Learn about the ship-wrecks that occurred along the Keys' reefs and the efforts to salvage these lost treasures.

Henry Flagler's Overseas Railway: Discover the ambitious vision of Henry Flagler, who extended his Florida East Coast Railway to Key West in the early 20th century. Explore the engineering marvel of the Overseas Railway, which connected the Keys to the mainland and transformed the islands' development.

The 1935 Labor Day Hurricane: Relive the devastating impact of the 1935 Labor Day Hurricane, one of the most powerful storms to ever hit the United States. Learn about the storm's destructive force, the lives lost, and the resilience of the Keys' community in rebuilding their lives and homes.

**Interactive exhibits and engaging displays:**

Immersive Experiences: The museum features interactive exhibits that bring history to life. Explore a replica of Indian Key, a once-thriving settlement that was destroyed by a hurricane in 1840. Step into a recreated 1930s general store and experience life in the Keys before the overseas highway.

Artifacts and Treasures: Discover a fascinating collection of artifacts, including archaeological finds from the Calusa era, shipwreck treasures, historical photographs, and personal belongings of early Key West settlers.

Educational Programs: The museum offers a variety of educational programs and events for all ages, including lectures, workshops, and guided tours. These programs provide a deeper understanding of the Keys' history, culture, and environment.

**Visitor Information:**

- Address: 82100 Overseas Highway, Islamorada, FL 33036
- Operating Hours: 10:00 AM to 5:00 PM, Tuesday through Sunday (closed Monday)
- Admission Fees:
  - Adults: $12

- Seniors (62+): $10
- Students (with valid ID): $8
- Youth (7-18 years): $6
- Children (6 & under): Free

- Accessibility: The museum is wheelchair accessible.
- Website: keysdiscovery.com

**Enhancing Your Museum Experience:**

Guided Tours: For a more in-depth understanding of the museum's collection and the Keys' history, guided tours are available. Led by knowledgeable docents, these tours offer valuable insights and enrich the visitor experience.

Special Exhibitions: The museum regularly hosts rotating special exhibitions, featuring specific aspects of the Keys' history, culture, or environment. Check the museum's website or inquire at the admissions desk for current and upcoming exhibitions.

Research Library: The Jerry Wilkinson Research Library, located on the second floor, offers a wealth of resources for those interested in delving deeper into the Keys' history.

The Florida Keys History & Discovery Centre is a must-visit for history buffs, nature lovers, and anyone curious about the fascinating stories that have shaped this unique island chain. Its engaging exhibits, interactive displays, and educational programs provide a captivating journey through time.

# Chapter 9: Beyond the Beach

## Eco-Tourism

The Florida Keys, a delicate archipelago teeming with biodiversity, beckon travelers with their pristine beauty and vibrant marine ecosystems. However, this fragile paradise demands a mindful approach to exploration. Embrace the principles of eco-tourism and embark on a journey that minimizes environmental impact while supporting local conservation efforts.

**Sustainable aquatic adventures:**

Navigating the Mangroves: Glide through tranquil mangrove forests by kayak or paddleboard, immersing yourself in this vital ecosystem without disturbing its delicate balance. Opt for outfitters committed to sustainable practices and educational initiatives that promote responsible interaction with this unique environment.

Coral Reef Conservation: Discover the underwater wonders of the coral reefs while adhering to eco-conscious practices. Utilize reef-safe sunscreen devoid of harmful chemicals, maintain a respectful distance from coral formations, and choose tour operators who prioritize sustainable diving and snorkeling practices. Consider participating in a reef clean-up initiative to actively contribute to the preservation of this vital ecosystem.

**Terrestrial Explorations with a Light Footprint:**

Wildlife Observation: Venture into wildlife refuges and rehabilitation centres, such as the National Key Deer Refuge, the Florida Keys Wild Bird Rehabilitation Centre, or the Turtle Hospital, to observe the unique fauna of the Keys and learn about ongoing conservation efforts. Maintain a respectful distance from wildlife, refrain from feeding them, and adhere to designated trails to minimize disturbance to their natural habitats.

Human-Powered Exploration: Opt for cycling or walking to explore the islands, reducing your carbon footprint while enjoying the scenic beauty at a leisurely pace. Utilize designated bike paths and walking trails to minimize impact on vegetation and wildlife habitats.

**Sustainable Practices for Conscious Travelers:**

Eco-Conscious Accommodations: Select accommodations that prioritize sustainability through initiatives such as solar power utilization, water conservation measures, and robust recycling programs. Seek out hotels and resorts with recognized green certifications or those actively engaged in local conservation partnerships. Minimize personal energy consumption by turning off lights and air conditioning when not in use, and consider reusing towels and linens to conserve water.

Supporting Local Stewardship: Patronize restaurants, shops, and tour operators that demonstrate a commitment to sustainable practices and contribute to the well-being of the local community. Prioritize businesses that source ingredients locally, utilize eco-friendly products, and actively participate in conservation initiatives. Minimize waste by utilizing reusable water bottles and shopping bags.

Minimizing Plastic Pollution: Join the Florida Keys' collective effort to combat plastic pollution. Carry reusable water bottles, straws, and utensils to reduce reliance on single-use plastics. Support businesses that offer eco-friendly alternatives and actively participate in beach clean-ups or volunteer with organizations dedicated to mitigating plastic pollution.

By embracing the principles of eco-tourism and making conscious choices during your travels, you contribute to the long-term preservation of the Florida Keys' natural splendor, ensuring that future generations can experience the magic of this island paradise.

# Festivals & Events

The Florida Keys are more than just beautiful beaches and stunning sunsets; they are also a vibrant hub of cultural celebrations, music festivals, sporting events, and unique local gatherings that take place throughout the year. Immerse yourself in the lively spirit of the islands and experience the diverse events that make the Keys a truly special destination.

**Cultural Celebrations:**

Fantasy Fest (Key West, October): This ten-day extravaganza is a celebration of creativity and self-expression, featuring elaborate costumes, lively parades, and themed parties. Embrace the spirit of fantasy and let your imagination run wild.

Hemingway Days (Key West, July): Celebrate the life and legacy of Ernest Hemingway, the iconic author who called Key West home for many years. This festival features a look-alike contest, literary readings, fishing tournaments, and a running of the bulls (with man-made bulls!).

Goombay Festival (Key West, February): Immerse yourself in the vibrant Bahraini culture of Key West at this lively street festival. Enjoy live music, dancing, authentic Bahamas food, and colorful costumes.

**Music Festivals:**

Key West Songwriters Festival (May): This renowned festival brings together some of the biggest names in song writing, showcasing their talents in intimate venues throughout Key West. Enjoy live performances, songwriter workshops, and a chance to connect with the creative minds behind your favorite songs.

Key Largo Original Music Festival (May): Discover talented musicians from across the country at this multi-day festival. Enjoy live performances in various venues throughout Key Largo, showcasing a diverse range of genres, from folk and blues to rock and reggae.

Underwater Music Festival (Looe Key Reef, July): This unique festival takes place underwater at Looe Key Reef, featuring music broadcast through underwater speakers. Snorkel or dive among the coral reefs and marine life while enjoying a symphony of ocean-themed tunes.

**Sporting Events:**

- Seven Mile Bridge Run (April): Challenge yourself with this iconic race across the Seven Mile Bridge, offering stunning views and a unique athletic experience.
- Key West Half Marathon & 5k (January): Run through the historic streets of key west and enjoy the scenic beauty of the island during this popular race.
- Cheeca Lodge Presidential Sailfish Tournament (Islamorada, January): Witness the excitement of this prestigious fishing tournament, attracting anglers from around the world to compete for the coveted title.

**Unique Local Gatherings:**

- Minimal Regatta (Key Largo, May): This quirky race features homemade boats constructed from unconventional materials, resulting in a hilarious and entertaining spectacle.
- Key West Conch Shell Blowing Contest (March): Test your lung capacity and compete in this light-hearted contest, a Key West tradition that celebrates the island's unique heritage.

- Pigeon Key Art Festival (Marathon, February): Browse and purchase unique artwork from local artists at this annual festival held on the historic island of Pigeon Key.

With its diverse calendar of events, the Florida Keys offer something for everyone throughout the year. Immerse yourself in the vibrant culture, enjoy the lively music, and experience the unique celebrations that make this island paradise a truly unforgettable destination.

# Responsible Travel

The Florida Keys are a treasure trove of natural beauty and unique ecosystems, but their delicate balance requires a mindful approach to tourism. By embracing responsible travel practices, you can help preserve the Keys' pristine environment and vibrant culture for generations to come. Here are some practical tips to minimize your impact and leave a positive footprint:

**Protecting the Marine Environment:**

- Reef-Safe Sunscreen: Choose sunscreen that is free of oxybenzone and octinoxate, chemicals that harm coral reefs. Seek out mineral-based sunscreens that include titanium dioxide or zinc oxide.
- Mindful Diving and Snorkeling: Maintain a safe distance from coral reefs, avoid touching or standing on them, and never feed marine life. Choose tour operators that

prioritize sustainable practices and educate guests about reef etiquette.

- Reduce plastic consumption: Bring your own reusable water bottle, straw, and utensils to minimize plastic waste. Avoid single-use plastics like bags and packaging whenever possible. Dispose of trash properly and participate in beach clean-ups if you see litter.

## Conserving Resources:

- Water Conservation: Take shorter showers, turn off the faucet while brushing your teeth, and reuse towels to conserve water, a precious resource in the Keys.
- Energy Efficiency: Turn off lights and air conditioning when leaving your accommodation. Choose accommodations that prioritize energy efficiency and sustainable practices.
- Transportation Choices: Consider walking, biking, or using public transportation to reduce your carbon footprint. If renting a car, choose a fuel-efficient model.

## Supporting Local Communities:

- Shop Local: Support local businesses, artisans, and restaurants to contribute to the local economy and preserve the unique character of the Keys.
- Respect Local Culture: Learn about the Keys' history and culture, and be mindful of local customs and traditions.

Respect the privacy of residents and avoid excessive noise.

- Volunteer Your Time: Consider volunteering with local organizations dedicated to environmental conservation or community development.

**Respecting Wildlife:**

- Observe from a Distance: Maintain a safe distance from wildlife and avoid feeding or disturbing them. For close views, use a telephoto lens or binoculars.
- Protect Nesting Sites: Be mindful of nesting sites for sea turtles, birds, and other wildlife. Avoid disturbing nests or hatchlings.
- Drive Carefully: Key deer and other wildlife often cross roads, especially at dawn and dusk. Be mindful of your surroundings and drive gently.

**Additional Tips:**

- Pack Light: Reduce your luggage weight to minimize fuel consumption during transportation.
- Choose Eco-Friendly Tours: select tour operators that prioritize sustainability and responsible practices.
- Educate Yourself: Learn about the environmental challenges facing the Florida Keys and how you can contribute to solutions.

By practicing responsible travel, you can help preserve the natural beauty and cultural heritage of the Florida Keys, ensuring that this unique destination remains a paradise for generations to come.

# Dear Reader

Thank you for choosing Florida Keys Travel Guide 2025 as your companion on this journey. I hope the insights, tips, and stories within these pages have enriched your experience and sparked a deeper love for Florida's rich culture and breath-taking landscapes.

Your feedback is invaluable to me. If you enjoyed this guide and found it helpful, I would greatly appreciate it if you could take a moment to leave a positive review. Your thoughts not only help other travelers discover this book but also inspire me to continue sharing the wonders of the world through my writing.

Thank you for being a part of this adventure. I wish you safe travels and unforgettable memories.

Warm regards,

*Glen C. Flores*

Made in United States
Troutdale, OR
04/10/2025

30502064R00082